WALKING
with
JESUS

WALKING *with* JESUS

Devotions for Advent & Christmas 2025

Editors of *Mornings with Jesus*
A GUIDEPOSTS DEVOTIONAL

Guideposts

A Gift from Guideposts

Thank you for your purchase! We want to express our gratitude for your support with a special gift just for you.

Dive into *Spirit Lifters*, a complimentary e-book that will fortify your faith, offering solace during challenging moments. Its 31 carefully selected scripture verses will soothe and uplift your soul.

Please use the QR code or go to **guideposts.org/spiritlifters** to download.

Walking with Jesus: Devotions for Advent & Christmas 2025
Editors of Guideposts

Published by Guideposts
100 Reserve Road, Suite E200
Danbury, CT 06810
Guideposts.org

Copyright © 2025 by Guideposts. All rights reserved.

This book, or parts thereof, may not be reproduced, stored in a retrieval system, or transmitted in any form or by any means, electronic, mechanical, photocopying, recording or otherwise, without the written permission of the publisher.

Cover and interior design by Pamela Walker, W Design Studio
Cover photo by Dreamstime
Typeset by Aptara, Inc.

ISBN 978-1-961442-73-3 (softcover)
ISBN 978-1-961442-74-0 (epub)

Printed and bound in the United States of America
10 9 8 7 6 5 4 3 2 1

Christmas Eve

Christmas hath a darkness
Brighter than the blazing noon,
Christmas hath a chillness
Warmer than the heat of June,
Christmas hath a beauty
Lovelier than the world can show:
For Christmas bringeth Jesus,
Brought for us so low.

Earth, strike up your music,
Birds that sing and bells that ring;
Heaven hath answering music
For all Angels soon to sing:
Earth, put on your whitest
Bridal robe of spotless snow:
For Christmas bringeth Jesus,
Brought for us so low.

Christina Rossetti

Introduction

Rejoice in the coming of Advent! Waiting isn't something most of us find pleasant, but certain things, especially the imminent arrival of a child, fill us with happy anticipation. And when that child is the one Son of God, sent expressly to save us, that joy is unfettered. *Walking with Jesus: Devotions for Advent & Christmas 2025* can help us prepare our hearts and faith to celebrate the great gift, our Lord's birth, and prepare us for His Second Coming.

The word *Advent*, which means "coming" or "arrival" in Latin, is never mentioned in the Bible, yet biblical accounts of that waiting are what Advent is all about. For centuries, the prophets of the Old Testament had foretold the coming of Jesus. As the prophet Isaiah declared generations before,

> "For to us a child is born.... And he will be called Wonderful Counselor, Mighty God, Everlasting Father, Prince of Peace."
> (Isaiah 9:6, NIV)

Anticipation of the Messiah's arrival had not faded by the era of Christ's earthly life. The shepherds may have been "terrified" by the appearance of the angel—who famously assured them, "Do not be afraid. I bring you good news that will cause great joy for all the people" (Luke 2:9–10, NIV)—but many people at that time were waiting expectantly for the Savior's appearance. The Bible also tells us that at least two people recognized the arrival of the young Jesus in Jerusalem for what it was: the introduction of Christ. The first of these was a "righteous and devout" man named Simeon. "It had been revealed to him by the Holy Spirit that he would not die before he had seen the Lord's Messiah" (Luke 2:25–26, NIV). He approached the Holy Family, took Jesus in his arms, and said,

> "Sovereign Lord, as you have promised,
> you may now dismiss your servant in peace.

> For my eyes have seen your salvation,
> which you have prepared in the sight of all nations:
> a light for revelation to the Gentiles,
> and the glory of your people Israel." (Luke 2:29–32, NIV)

The other mention is shorter but no less intriguing. A prophet named Anna recognized the tiny child's true identity and made her way to Mary and Joseph while they were in Jerusalem.

"She was very old; she had lived with her husband seven years after her marriage, and then was a widow until she was eighty-four. She never left the temple but worshiped night and day, fasting and praying. Coming up to them at that very moment, she gave thanks to God and spoke about the child to all who were looking forward to the redemption of Jerusalem" (Luke 2:36–38, NIV).

The Bible tells us that Joseph and Mary were left in wonderment by these prophecies. Their fulfillment would take many years, as all would be revealed in God's time. Our Advent wait is, thankfully, much, much shorter.

The 2025 Advent calendar begins on Sunday, November 30. As time ticks toward the blessed arrival of our Lord, let us spiritually prepare ourselves for Christmas and for our obligations as Christians. As Dr. Norman Vincent Peale, cofounder of Guideposts, once said, "Christmas is a time of renewal. Pause and ask yourself: How obedient am I to God's Will and His Word? None of us is perfect in this regard. But when defiance or rebellion or selfish impulses come crowding in, it might help to remember an honest, uncomplaining carpenter named Joseph, and try to follow the example he has left us."

The devotions in this book draw us away from the holiday's busyness and the distractions and the troubles of the world and toward the long arc of our redemption and reunion with the Almighty. Each Sunday of Advent has a theme that draws from the teachings of Christ—hope, peace, joy, and love. In *Walking with Jesus: Devotions for Advent & Christmas 2025*, these themes set the tone for the week's devotions that follow. As we happily anticipate the many blessings of the season—the community and the cheer—we recount the story behind it: our Savior's birth. On this quest, our trusted writers help us by providing three devotions—first-person stories of spiritual resonance—for each day leading up to Christmas. Accompanying them are a scripture quote and a faith step, which can help you apply the lesson to your daily life. You may choose to read the devotions all at once or parcel them out through your day and week as you would with an Advent calendar. There's also dedicated space at the back of the book for you to share your impressions and memories of the season.

As we wait for Jesus's triumphant return, Advent gives us an opportunity to prepare and practice our love for Jesus. With this birth, God proved His great and sustaining love for a flawed humanity by sending and redeeming us through His Son. Each aspect of Advent that we celebrate is an affirmation of that momentous gift as well as an opportunity to reengage with Christ as God reengaged with us. May we reach toward His outstretched hand and step forward on that journey with hope, peace, joy, and love.

Lisa Guernsey

Hope

O holy night! The stars are brightly shining;
  It is the night of the dear Savior's birth.
Long lay the world in sin and error pining,
Till He appeared and the soul felt its worth.
A thrill of hope—the weary world rejoices,
For yonder breaks a new and glorious morn!
Fall on your knees! O hear the angel voices!
O night divine, O night when Christ was born!
O night, O holy night, O night divine!

First Sunday of Advent, November 30

*I wait for the LORD, my whole being waits, and in his word
I put my hope. Psalm 130:5 (NIV)*

WHILE ORDERING MY CHRISTMAS GIFTS online last year, I spent so much money that the retailer offered me a desk lamp for free. Oddly, I had just set up a new workstation in the corner of my living room and the area was dark. I couldn't wait for that light to arrive to brighten my space.

Over the next few weeks, package after package arrived, none of which contained that lamp. Still, I waited with hopeful anticipation for what would illuminate my desk, making it easier for me to work. I'd no longer have to exert my eyes to see what was before me. Finally, it arrived! I rushed to plug it in, and, voilà! That lamp truly does light up my corner workstation, making my desk so much brighter.

Like my freely given lamp, Jesus gives Himself freely too, and His divine light will pierce the darkness soon. We don't have to strive to earn His love or prove ourselves worthy in any way, we only have to believe. Just as we keep an eye out at the mailbox, front door, or driveway for deliveries, we need to keep the eyes of our heart looking, seeking, and waiting with hope. When Jesus does arrive, He'll illuminate the corners of our heart, mind, and world. Receiving Him with open arms will help us see more clearly all the other gifts before us, the ones He blesses us with all year through.
—CLAIRE MCGARRY

FAITH STEP: *Sit near a lamp and consider what you're hoping for this season. When you see the mailman or a delivery driver pull up, imagine that hope being delivered directly to you.*

ADVENT DAY 1 MIDDAY

First Sunday of Advent, November 30

Why, my soul, are you downcast? Why so disturbed within me? Put your hope in God, for I will yet praise him, my Savior and my God. Psalm 42:11 (NIV)

IN THINKING ABOUT MY COUNTENANCE in terms of color, at this time of year, my spirit usually felt poinsettia red and Christmas tree green—bright with hope. But a hard year had faded the brilliance into more muted tones. My mom's health had declined rapidly in the spring, causing her to bounce between hospitals and rehab centers for several months. She went to be with Jesus in June.

I opened the Christian radio app on my phone, now playing around-the-clock holiday favorites. I sang along with cheerful tunes and tried to recapture the wonder of the season. Then, an old, familiar carol began. "O come, all ye faithful, joyful and triumphant! O come ye, O come ye to Bethlehem."

Though I'd heard the song all my life, two words stood out to me for the first time: joyful and triumphant. What beautiful messages those adjectives represented, messages I needed to hear. I had allowed the worries of my world to change "joyful and triumphant" to "downcast and defeated." The song invited me to return to Bethlehem, look upon the manger, and find refreshed hope through the birth of baby Jesus.

I raised the music volume and lifted my voice in praise. "O come, let us adore Him; O come, let us adore Him; O come, let us adore Him, Christ, the Lord!" Once again, my spirit radiated like red poinsettias and glowed like the green of my Christmas tree.
—BECKY ALEXANDER

FAITH STEP: *On this first Sunday of Advent, listen to or sing "O Come, All Ye Faithful." Focus your thoughts on the hope Jesus brings, regardless of circumstances.*

First Sunday of Advent, November 30

> But when the set time had fully come,
> God sent his Son. Galatians 4:4 (NIV)

I DISCOVERED A 52-WEEK SAVINGS plan that totaled $1,378 by year's end. Save one dollar in week one, two dollars in week two, and on through all 52 weeks. I followed the plan week after week as a surprise for my husband.

Over dinner at the end of the year, I slid an envelope across the table with the cash I'd been scrimping and stashing away. He was amazed. We repeated the savings year after year, and he used it for his dream hunting trip to Argentina for a significant birthday.

We decided to save for my big birthday trip next. We've accomplished that, and the birthday came and went two years ago. But I've put off the trip because I haven't decided where to go and it never seems like the right time. I've leaned into such excuses as I can't make up my mind, and my teenagers and their schedules need me. Honestly, I've had the place narrowed down for a while (the English countryside) and my kids will be fine.

I've enjoyed the anticipation, but lately my inclination to stop waiting and go sounds like a friendly nagging voice in my head. It is time to move past anticipation and act.

Advent holds anticipation that leads to something big—Jesus's birthday. I'm so grateful the time came for His Father to move past humanity's anticipation and send Jesus as our Savior.
—ERIN KEELEY MARSHALL

FAITH STEP: *Make your own advent calendar. It can be a simple checkbox or something ornate. As you enjoy this month of anticipation and Advent's miraculous finale, thank Jesus for His willingness to act in the perfect way and time.*

ADVENT DAY 2 MORNING

Monday, December 1

Every good gift and every perfect gift is from above, and comes down from the Father of lights, with whom there is no variation or shadow of turning. James 1:17 (NKJV)

WHEN I WAS A CHILD, Christmas was an annual, uneventful event. My parents would fill my stocking with oranges, nuts, and a piece of candy, and my grandmother would give me a gift of socks and underwear. I never asked for any of these things. Ever. Apparently my loved ones considered these items essential to life, and as a result, I was blessed every Christmas with clean knickers, fresh socks, and healthy snacks. I could count on it!

In a small way, my family modeled what my Heavenly Father did for me when He sent His Son to earth. I never asked for Jesus to be born in one of the most humble of fashions. Or for Him to live a sacrificial life that paved the way for me to live an abundant one. Jesus came to give me what I never asked for or could never have paid for myself—salvation (John 3:16). My family's gifts were temporary essentials, but my Savior's gift was eternally essential. I could count on both—the extravagant love of Jesus as well as those juicy oranges, mixed nuts, and fresh Fruit of the Looms! —KRISTEN WEST

FAITH STEP: *What organization would cherish essentials? Hygiene items to a shelter? A check to your favorite nonprofit? Whatever you do, add something extravagant to reflect what Jesus has done for you.*

Monday, December 1

These commandments that I give you today are to be on your hearts. Impress them on your children. Talk about them when you sit at home and when you walk along the road, when you lie down and when you get up. Tie them as symbols on your hands and bind them on your foreheads. Write them on the doorframes of your houses and on your gates. Deuteronomy 6:6–9 (NIV)

Our favorite steak restaurant in Houston is well-known for its elaborate Christmas decorations. Each year, the entire restaurant goes through a total transformation from its everyday Texas-themed decor to gorgeous holiday-themed embellishments that adorn every inch of the walls and waiting areas.

This year I was thrilled to discover a new addition to the festivities: a collection of more than one hundred expertly crafted Steinbach nutcrackers beautifully displayed in one room of the restaurant. While we waited for a table, I explored the details of each, and I couldn't help but calculate the cost of such an investment. I doubted I'd ever purchase a nutcracker from such a world-famous craftsman, much less dozens.

Then I remembered an article I read about the owners of the restaurant, and their design choices made more sense. The article said they consider the restaurant their mission field, and they begin each day by walking through every room and praying for their employees and customers. For them, their Christmas decorations are part of their strategic ministry. They infuse their restaurant with beauty to bless the community and to honor Jesus for how He's blessed their business. I'd like my Christmas decorations, whether humble or elaborate, to do the same. —Emily E. Ryan

Faith Step: *Find a Christmas decoration that points people to Jesus and display it prominently, for all to see.*

Monday, December 1

If I go up to the heavens, you are there. If I lie down in the grave, you are there. If I rise with the sun in the east and settle in the west beyond the sea, even there you would guide me. With your right hand you would hold me. Psalm 139:8–10 (NCV)

When my children were young, our family traveled to visit extended family at Christmas. After our kids moved away in different directions, my husband's job changes brought a few relocations for us. Christmas included even more travel: either airline flights or a two-week road trip of a few thousand miles, with stays in several different homes, hotels, and/or rentals. The radio may have been playing, "Oh, there's no place like home for the holidays," but I had learned to pack Christmas up and take it with me.

My favorite version of *A Christmas Carol* is the 1999 movie starring Patrick Stewart. I love the scene when the Ghost of Christmas Present takes Scrooge to different locations where "Silent Night" is being sung: a poor cottage in England, a remote lighthouse high on a rocky cliff, a ship bouncing around on stormy seas, and a place where workers were emerging from an underground coal mine.

Christmas doesn't depend on being where I want to be, or even on observing cherished traditions. Christmas happens whenever I honor the birth of my Savior, the One who promises to be with me no matter where I am—geographically, emotionally, or spiritually. He is always with me. —Dianne Neal Matthews

Faith Step: *Take out paper and pen and read Psalm 139:1–18. List any places where Jesus would not be with you. (Since your page is blank, draw a big heart with His name inside.)*

Tuesday, December 2

Brothers and sisters, we do not want you to be uninformed about those who sleep in death, so that you do not grieve like the rest of mankind, who have no hope. 1 Thessalonians 4:13 (NIV)

I PICKED UP THE BOX of ornaments, struggling to hold back tears. This was the first Christmas without my grandmother, and decorating the tree was one of her favorite things about the holiday. I had a few boxes of her Christmas decorations, so to keep her memory alive, I decided to place her ornaments on the tree first. I unwrapped an ornament with an image of the Montreal skyline, a gift I'd given her shortly after I moved to the city, and hung it on a limb. There were also framed photos of her children and grandchildren. I remembered asking her why she felt the need to scatter her family members on her tree's limbs. "If they can't be with me physically, I like to think they are here in spirit," she said, engulfing me in a big bear hug.

Whether it is the first holiday or many years have passed since losing a loved one, navigating Christmas without their presence is difficult. But I cling to the hope that one day, I will see my grandmother again. Until that time comes, I'll cherish the hand-painted bauble and the rest of her ornaments knowing Grandma is here in spirit. —LAURA BAILEY

FAITH STEP: *Have you lost a loved one this year? Place a commemorative ornament on the tree or find something to do that keeps their spirit alive this season.*

Tuesday, December 2

But Jesus called the children to him and said, "Let the little children come to me, and do not hinder them, for the kingdom of God belongs to such as these." Luke 18:16 (NIV)

I LOVINGLY LIFTED MY CHERISHED ceramic sculpture of Mary, Joseph, and the baby Jesus from the closet. A gift from years back, the vibrantly painted figures took my breath away each time I looked at it. Mary's and Joseph's expressions reflected awe as the baby raised outstretched arms toward them. Every year, this Nativity was the first thing I set out at Christmas and the last thing I put away. Did I dare risk displaying it this year, with my young grandchildren coming for a visit? If they broke it, my heart would break too. The thundering of small hooves signaled the arrival of the four kids, ages two, three, four, and five. Having seen them successfully dismantle a house in ten minutes, I headed them off at the pass, intending to divert them to the toy room, but something, Someone, stopped me.

"Kids, come see," I said, as I led them to the table. "This is the baby Jesus and His mommy and daddy." I gave them a mini version of the Christmas story, and then, throwing caution to the wind, I invited them to touch the sculpture. Chubby fingers gently caressed each figure in the Nativity, and then they were off to the toy room. My heart soared!

I vowed to worry less about breaking my statue and more about building my grandkids' faith. —PAT BUTLER DYSON

FAITH STEP: *Ask Jesus to place people in your life, including children, with whom you can share His story.*

Tuesday, December 2

This was how the birth of Jesus Christ took place. Matthew 1:18 (GNT)

HUBBY AND I ARE BECOMING experts on the Christmas movie genre. We even created a laminated, bingo-like game card with forty-eight common Christmas movie clichés, such as an engagement, travel, small town, opening gifts, pickup truck, gingerbread house, Christmas pajamas, ugly Christmas sweater, a mean neighbor, a Christmas miracle. Upon spotting these clichés while watching Christmas movies, we cross them off our game card with a dry erase marker.

Sadly, most Christmas movies completely miss the whole point of Christmas. Conversely, when we watched *The Nativity Story*, not surprisingly, the movie didn't seem to have any of the stereotypical Christmas movie clichés. But, as I looked at my laminated card, I began to notice some things. There was an engagement (Mary and Joseph), travel (from Nazareth), a small town (Bethlehem), gifts (from the Wise Men). There wasn't a pickup truck, but there was a donkey, which Mary rode to Bethlehem. There wasn't a gingerbread house but another unusual structure: a stable, where Jesus was born. There weren't festive pajamas or an ugly Christmas sweater, but there were swaddling cloths, wrapped around baby Jesus. There wasn't a mean neighbor; but there was a mean king who wanted to kill the baby. And there were Christmas miracles upon miracles (an angel appeared to Mary, Immaculate Conception, God born as a baby). Recognizing these correlations, I now have a deeper understanding of the sacred symbolism of the Nativity story tucked into Christmas movies. Clichés aside, I pray I'll stay focused on the real point of Christmas—remembering the birth of Jesus. —CASSANDRA TIERSMA

FAITH STEP: *Put on a Christmas sweater or festive pajamas, make some popcorn, and watch your favorite Christmas movie. Look for symbols of Jesus amidst the usual Christmas movie clichés.*

ADVENT DAY 4 MORNING

WEDNESDAY, DECEMBER 3

For by one sacrifice he has made perfect forever those who are being made holy. Hebrews 10:14 (NIV)

SOMETIMES I WONDER WHAT IT would be like to have more than one earthly life. What would I do with a second path?

It might be nice to grow up in a different part of the world. I'd explore a new vocation or educational setting, like a college on a coast. Maybe I'd choose a career in interior design or travel vlogging.

And maybe characteristics I've wished to tweak in myself wouldn't be annoyances. If I could choose, I'd be less prone to people pleasing and better at chitchat. I'd be more gracious with myself, and I'd have a stronger mind for business.

It's a curiosity to me that God chose one earthly life for a human being. And one Jesus as Savior.

I love the life I have and seeing Jesus's presence in the details. But I can still be curious about His decision making. These things keep my brain stirring!

During Advent my curiosity mellows into quiet wonder at the One who knows all and sees all.

Jesus's one life on earth makes all the difference for mine. Otherwise, I wouldn't receive the eternal extension with Him in heaven that will miraculously make up for lingering wishes about the here and now.

One day, I'll be with Jesus in person. My second path, or eternal life, will begin and I'll look in His eyes and understand why He's the One worthy of all my worship on earth and in heaven.
—ERIN KEELEY MARSHALL

FAITH STEP: *On a sheet of paper draw a lifeline and list significant moments and where you were with Jesus when each occurred. Thank Him for the path you've traveled and the future He offers.*

WEDNESDAY, DECEMBER 3

Jesus replied, "Foxes have dens, and birds have nests. But the Son of Man doesn't have a place to call his own." Matthew 8:20 (CEV)

FOR DECADES, I'VE LONGED TO host someone besides the members of our small family for our holiday feast. Someone who couldn't afford to reciprocate. Someone who was alone. Someone who needed a family—even for merely one day—to help them feel seen and valued and loved.

A couple weeks before Christmas, our granddaughter Grace asked me if she could invite her friend Dori to have Christmas dinner with us. "I'd love to have Dori," I told Grace. "But does she not have a family?"

"She can't live with her family, Grandma. But she's my age, only seventeen! The homeless ministry rents an apartment for her so she can stay in school."

My heart broke for Dori. Although our town is small, we have many homeless teens due to drug abuse issues in their families. Hopes and Dreams, funded by a thrift store and donations, is a ministry that helps teens experiencing homelessness find shelter. Now Jesus was giving us the opportunity to have one of those teens sit at our table for Christmas. If not for the reason behind Dori's situation, I would've clapped and cheered that my Christmas hostess dream had finally come true.

As the two girls chatted while they feasted, I thanked Jesus that He'd arranged to have a sweet young guest join us. I also thanked Him for leaving His glorious, elegant home in heaven to become an itinerant preacher who relied on the hospitality of others during much of His time on earth. —JEANETTE LEVELLIE

FAITH STEP: *Consider hosting a forgotten person at your table. Serve your most-loved recipes on your best dishes.*

ADVENT DAY 4 EVENING

WEDNESDAY, DECEMBER 3

We are filled with hope, as we wait for the glorious return of our great God and Savior Jesus Christ. Titus 2:13 (CEV)

THE WEEKS BETWEEN THANKSGIVING AND Christmas zip by in a flash—so much to plan, decorate, buy, wrap, cook, and attend. I often marvel at how that same time period dragged on forever during my childhood. Despite my impatience, I never doubted what Christmas morning would bring: a few toys that I'd circled in the Sears catalog along with other surprises, a special meal, and time spent with extended family. As difficult as the waiting seemed to my immature mind, Christmas morning was always worth it.

The old adage "Good things come to those who wait" is a principle expressed throughout the Bible. Luke shares a perfect example (2:22–38). Forty days after Jesus's birth, Mary and Joseph traveled to Jerusalem for the prescribed rites. Simeon was a devout Jew who had been promised by God that he would not die before he saw the Messiah. He entered the temple and immediately recognized the baby as the One he'd waited for. Anna, an elderly widow who stayed at the temple praying and fasting, walked up as Simeon was praising God. She joined in and later spread the news about Jesus to others who were looking forward to the promised Messiah.

When this earthly life seems hard, I can look ahead to seeing my Redeemer face-to-face in His perfect timing. Like Simeon and Anna, I expect to break out in spontaneous praise and rejoicing. For now, the waiting may be difficult, but I know it will be worth it. —DIANNE NEAL MATTHEWS

FAITH STEP: *Read the story of Simeon and Anna. Talk to Jesus about your own waiting. What does your heart most long to see?*

Thursday, December 4

I praise you for remembering me in everything and for holding to the traditions just as I passed them on to you. 1 Corinthians 11:2 (NIV)

My mom's house was silent as I gazed out her living room window. Her neighbor's homes were decorated with dancing lights and oversized inflatables in the yards. Christmas was less than a week away, but for Mom and me, there would be few festivities.

Mom lay in bed and slept most of the day, her memories lost to Alzheimer's. As her sole caregiver, I prayed that somehow, Mom could recognize it was Christmas. I'd sung carols and read the Christmas story from the Bible, but nothing I did seemed to reach her.

Two days before Christmas, a large package arrived from my brother. It was a live, three-foot-tall pine tree. The package contained colorful lights and ornaments. There were deer ornaments, pinecones, and even an angel for the top. The card read, "May the miracle of our Lord's birth surround you with love."

I took the tree into Mom's bedroom. After placing it on a corner table, I plugged in the lights. A warm glow surrounded Mom's room. I turned suddenly, thinking I had heard a noise. Mom's eyes were alert and bright as she looked at the tree. She repeated what I thought I had heard. The single word "Oh" broke through. I squeezed her hand.

Maybe Mom remembered after all. —Jeannie Hughes

Faith Step: *If you are a caregiver or around older loved ones, think of ways you might be able to connect with them and share Jesus's love.*

Thursday, December 4

Being confident of this, that he who began a good work in you will carry it on to completion until the day of Christ Jesus. Philippians 1:6 (NIV)

IT'S A TRADITION WE STARTED years ago. Every Christmas, my family knows that one of the packages sitting under our tree will be a box-in-a-box-in-a-box. No one (except me) knows who the special recipient of the package will be. But, once this much-anticipated present has been handed to the chosen person and they begin unwrapping, it quickly becomes apparent that this is *the* gift—the one where they'll have multiple layers to unwrap before getting to the actual present itself. My family absolutely loves this tradition, and our living room erupts with laughter and applause once the layered gift has been discovered.

My walk with Jesus includes layers of unwrapping, as well. Over the course of my life, trusting Jesus helps me continue to gently unwrap layers of worries—from being afraid of the dark to scared of being alone or wondering if my prodigal child would ever return. With each layer, Jesus reminds me that I am His and that His promised work is continuing in me. A life with Jesus—isn't that the real gift? —KRISTEN WEST

FAITH STEP: *Consider wrapping a Christmas present in several layers this year. As you do, remember the work Jesus continues to do in you and thank Him for it.*

Thursday, December 4

"In the same way, I tell you, there is rejoicing in the presence of the angels of God over one sinner who repents." Luke 15:10 (NIV)

I STEPPED OUT MY BACK door and snuggled into a chair with a blanket. Breathing in the crisp December evening, I sighed as I glanced up at the stars hanging brightly in the night sky. Scattered for all to see, their proximity reminded me of my cousins, whom I missed dearly. At one time, the eleven of us lived only a few hours' drive from each other, but marriage or employment had called each of us to relocate. Ohio. Alabama. Texas. Massachusetts. Oregon. And myself, in Pennsylvania. It had been too many Christmases since we'd all been together.

Yes, distance played a part, but if I were honest with myself, and Jesus, much of the blame for the lack of contact between my cousins and me was mine to bear. After I estranged myself from my father several years back, I failed to foster the relationships with those on his side of the family. I prayed for them often but felt awkward reaching out. Yet I could feel Jesus calling me to do so.

One of the flickering stars caught my eye. It seemed to dim and then disappear from the sky for a time, only to reappear brighter moments later. I knew what I had to do. Pledging to purchase additional Christmas cards, I hoped my handwritten holiday greetings (and apology for being absent) would warm their hearts and shine some reconciliation on our relationships. —GLORIA JOYCE

FAITH STEP: *Do you have a friend or family member with whom you have lost touch? Reach out today with a phone call or a card to show them you care.*

ADVENT DAY 6 MORNING

Friday, December 5

May the God of hope fill you with all joy and peace as you trust in him, so that you may overflow with hope by the power of the Holy Spirit. Romans 15:13 (NIV)

CHRISTMASTIME HAS ALWAYS BEEN A glorious season of purposeful planning and tradition for me, a period to share my affection with others through calls, hugs, and gifts. Fingerprints of love smudge my refrigerator and smears of happiness streak the kitchen, evidence of the baking I've done. Wrap and ribbons adorn the table with carefree abandon.

But this year was different. My husband, David, was ill. No decorations brightened our home, no garlands festooned the porch, no colorfully lit tree defied the darkness of winter. And no Nativity rested on our hearth to remind me of the perfect miracle of Jesus's birth.

Yet sitting alone in the semidarkness of a predawn morning, I felt Jesus's presence, and the downy blanket of His peace spread over me. From the quiet stillness of daybreak, the sun rose and with it came the promise of a better day. Hope welled within. I turned my head toward the bedroom and saw David's form filling the doorway, a gentle smile on his face. Even in the early light, I could tell he felt better. I bowed my head in a quick prayer of thanks, then hurried to wrap him in an embrace.

Christmastime is still a glorious season, when God opened the heavens to share His Son—the greatest source of hope—with us. And whether found in joyous celebrations or the quiet warmth of a treasured embrace, my heart overflows with it. —HEIDI GAUL

FAITH STEP: *Rise early tomorrow to witness the sunrise with prayer. Remember Jesus is here today and every day, to bring warmth, light, and especially hope.*

Friday, December 5

And we know that in all things God works for the good of those who love him, who have been called according to his purpose. Romans 8:28 (NIV)

EACH YEAR WHEN WE ARRIVE at my parents' house for Christmas, my mom has a new puzzle waiting for us on the dining room table. This year's puzzle was difficult—so many muted colors and tiny pieces. But Mom is tenacious. She always starts with the edges.

Over the next few days, I saw clusters of cousins circling the table looking perplexed. I sat in on one puzzling session. I couldn't find the right fit for the pieces I was looking for. I got frustrated, gave up, and read a book instead. Little by little, the puzzle came together. More than once, someone said, "I think we are missing a piece." The puzzling stopped until the errant piece was found. Several batches of cookies were consumed in the making of the puzzle. Then came the fantastic finish. The final piece was placed. A cheer went up! It all made sense now.

Jesus looks at the puzzle of my life, and it all makes sense to Him. The crazy middle pieces. The rough edges. The straight lines. He is not perplexed by my hodge-podge of good experiences, broken dreams, and wild mess-ups. Every high and low moment has its place. I can trust Him with the pieces because I know in His great love and sovereignty, He is working all things together for my good. —SUSANNA FOTH AUGHTMON

FAITH STEP: *What pieces of your life have you frustrated? Write them out and post them on your fridge. Ask Jesus to help you trust Him to work all things together for your good.*

Friday, December 5

So they hurried off and found Mary and Joseph, and the baby, who was lying in the manger. Luke 2:16 (NIV)

When I was young, my mother and aunt organized an informal Christmas pageant in my grandparents' living room. I had enough cousins for all the traditional roles to be filled—shepherds, wise men, sheep, angels, and the holy family. My youngest cousin was wrapped in a blanket for his breakout role as baby Jesus and laid in his car seat that was designated our makeshift manger. The rest of us scavenged linen closets for sheets and towels that could serve as costumes. We lined up in a back bedroom ready to begin our journey to Bethlehem via the long hallway that led to the living room where the adults were gathered.

My aunt began reading the Christmas story from Luke 2 while my mom worked as stage manager ushering us each onto the scene when it was our turn. My cousin Nathan and I were instructed to lock arms as Mary and Joseph as we walked solemnly down the corridor. Once everyone had joined us in our holy huddle, the story concluded and we sang traditional Christmas hymns as a family.

Now that I'm an adult, I would refer to that night as what some call a "core memory." The details have somewhat faded, but the feelings and significance certainly have not. Acting out the events of Jesus's birth ensured that the Christmas story was etched in my heart at an early age, and I think that's part of the beauty of the story itself. It is simple enough for a child to understand. —Emily E. Ryan

Faith Step: *Read Luke 2 aloud or make plans to act out the Christmas story with friends or family.*

SATURDAY, DECEMBER 6

And she brought forth her firstborn son, and wrapped him in swaddling clothes, and laid him in a manger; because there was no room for them in the inn. Luke 2:7 (KJV)

PULLING CHRISTMAS DECORATIONS OUT OF the garage, my husband, Matt, and I discovered damage to the box storing our artificial tree. Evidently, mice we trapped last spring had ruined it, but our budget did not have room for a new one. I placed our Nativity on a small table near the spot we usually put the tree. In a hardware store the week before Christmas, I longingly looked at the trees on display. The selection was large in both size and cost, but when an associate happened by, I asked if he had something smaller and on sale. He smiled and hurried to the rear of the store. Moments later, he brought out a tree less extravagant than their current inventory. It was supposed to be part of a window display, but they'd run out of room. He offered it to me for almost nothing, saying that it made his day to brighten ours.

That evening, my family cheered as multicolored light filled our living room once more. I scooted the Nativity scene beneath the tree with my eye on the innkeeper figurine. By choosing to make room for the Holy Family with an unusual solution, his act of hospitality brought light to the whole world. I sent up a prayer for today's shopkeeper who did the same for mine. —GLORIA JOYCE

FAITH STEP: *Imagine yourself like the innkeeper. Ask Jesus to show you a family and brighten their holiday in an unexpected way.*

SATURDAY, DECEMBER 6

John the Baptist came, preaching...saying, "Repent, for the kingdom of heaven has come near." Matthew 3:1–2 (NASB)

AS JOHN PREPARED THE WAY for Jesus, he called folks to a reset—an opportunity to see differently. Seeing differently leads to doing differently. And each of us doing differently, little by little, changes the world.

My favorite Christmas carol is "O Holy Night." That song contains the whole of my theology.

"O holy night! The stars are brightly shining; It is the night of our dear Savior's birth. Long lay the world in sin and error pining, Till He appeared, and the soul felt its worth."

Immanuel, God with us (Matthew 1:23), arrived in the darkest season on earth. That's when the Light of the World (John 8:12) chose to show up. And what He showed us by showing up is our worth. That's the perspective change John the Baptist invites us into.

If the "what" of the Christian story is "God with us," the "how" is found in the third verse of "O Holy Night": "Truly He taught us to love one another; His law is love and His gospel is peace. Chains shall He break, for the slave is our brother, And in His name all oppression shall cease." I believe when a soul really feels its worth, everything changes. We realize the worth within us is also the worth of everyone else around us. And we have a hope we can offer, if we are willing, and that can change the world. —GWEN FORD FAULKENBERRY

FAITH STEP: *Look in the mirror and say these affirmations of truth: I have great worth. I have hope. I can change the world.*

SATURDAY, DECEMBER 6

Those who are wise will shine like the brightness of the heavens, and those who lead many to righteousness, like the stars for ever and ever. Daniel 12:3 (NIV)

MY DAUGHTER, CHRISTINA, AND I often reminisce over Christmases long ago. One of our favorite memories involves the two of us out one evening, shopping for gifts. Pausing at an intersection, seven-year-old Christina gazed into the night sky and gasped. She'd spotted something small slowly trekking across the sky, quite obviously not a plane or helicopter. But what could it be? We attacked the question with as much logic and reasoning as possible and decided it could only have been Santa and his reindeer. This conclusion reassured Christina in Santa's existence, which by her age had become an object of great debate. To this day, with a wink and a smile, we say, "Maybe, just maybe..."

Years have passed, and Christina is now a wonderful, faith-filled woman. Gone are the fairy tales of childhood, replaced by a God so real, so far beyond our reasoning that we have no choice but to bow down in humble praise. As she and I stand together under the night sky, our eyes no longer search for a dimly lit sleigh. Instead, we remember the star that pointed to Jesus. A star so brilliant, wise men followed it to a stable in Bethlehem and our Savior. In the quiet darkness, we give thanks. And maybe, just maybe, when we ask Jesus to lend us His light, we will shine just as brightly, as we point others to Him. —HEIDI GAUL

FAITH STEP: *Spend some time outside tonight and search for the brightest star. Thank Jesus that you can be like that star and point others to Him.*

PEACE

Silent night, holy night,
All is calm, all is bright
Round yon virgin mother and child!
Holy Infant so tender and mild,
Sleep in heavenly peace,
Sleep in heavenly peace.

Silent night, holy night,
Darkness flies, all is light;
Shepherds hear the angels sing,
"Alleluia! Hail the King!
Christ the Savior is born,
Christ the Savior is born."

Second Sunday of Advent, December 7

> *"I have told you these things, so that in me you may have peace. In this world you will have trouble. But take heart! I have overcome the world."* John 16:33 (NIV)

WHEN I HEAR JESUS BEING hailed as the Prince of Peace at Christmastime, the lyrics from a familiar song from my childhood always attach themselves to the declaration like tinsel on a Christmas tree: "I've got peace like a river. I've got peace like a river." When I was young, the lyrics felt like a lullaby and a promise. I imagined gliding through life with Jesus like two lovers in a canoe rowing slowly toward the moonlight. Nothing rocking the boat. No ripples to navigate. But that's not at all how life unfolded, and it took time for me to reconcile my expectations with reality.

For our tenth anniversary, my husband and I went white water rafting in Tennessee. The river was unpredictable and tumultuous, and I felt small and vulnerable. As our guide maneuvered our raft through class IV rapids, I remembered those lyrics and again questioned the accuracy of comparing peace in Jesus to a river. But then my gaze found our guide's face. She was calm, focused, and in complete control. Even as I cried out in fear and distress, she remained steady and unshaken. I finally understood what peace on earth really means. It's not that I have the promise of still waters. It's that I have the promise of a peaceful spirit within rough waters as long as Jesus, my Prince of Peace, is my guide. —EMILY E. RYAN

FAITH STEP: *Sketch a boat with you and Jesus inside and your conflicts on the outside as if they are waves. Thank Jesus for guiding you smoothly through.*

Second Sunday of Advent, December 7

"Peace I leave with you; my peace I give you." John 14:27 (NIV)

I WATCH AS THE SECOND candle is lit on our church's Advent wreath. The flame made the purple candle of peace glow brightly. Looking at the light reminded me how friends say, "Protect your peace," when leaving church. I want to ask them how I'm supposed to protect something I don't have.

Peace is often hard to come by for me. Too often I allow others into my life who try to steal it. I can't make the whole world a more positive place, but I can start with myself. I try to remember to protect my peace when things aren't going right: my neighbor being angry when my tree drops leaves in his yard; losing my temper because my son has once again ignored his curfew.

I look back at the peace candle and remember the promises God made through my faith. When angels appeared, they proclaimed peace to the shepherds (Luke 2:14). When we greet others in church, we proclaim, "Peace be with you."

The flame from the purple candle glows brightly. It is my beacon. I know, from now on, I will try harder to protect my peace and concentrate on the peace Jesus brings me. —JEANNIE HUGHES

FAITH STEP: *List on a sheet of paper the reasons you are not at peace. After praying over each one, think of ways you could rectify the situation so that you may experience peace.*

Second Sunday of Advent, December 7

Now may the Lord of peace himself give you peace at all times and in every way. The Lord be with all of you. 2 Thessalonians 3:16 (NIV)

THIS CHRISTMAS SEASON, MY TALL bookcase adjacent to my desk is housing my ceramic Nativity. It brings me so much happiness. Mary and Joseph are in the stable adoring Jesus in the manger. The shepherds are beaming down at the baby King surrounded by some placid sheep and a very earnest-looking cow.

At the far end of the bookcase, I placed the three wise men and their camels. Behind them is a large metal star fitted with small light bulbs. I love plugging it in and illuminating this peaceful scene.

But my Nativity is nothing like the first Christmas. It was anything but peaceful. Mary and Joseph made their way to Bethlehem for a census on the heels of a scandal. She was an unwed mother. They were homeless. Mary gave birth far away from her family surrounded by livestock. It was a night filled with pain, stress, and chaos. But on that wild, holy night something shifted. A heavenly choir lit up the sky singing this deep truth: peace had finally come to earth.

This truth still rings out across the cosmos. When Jesus showed up, His presence shifted everything, bringing light into darkness, healing into suffering, and calm into chaos. Whatever struggle I face, He offers hope. In His presence, I don't have to worry. There is deep rest for my soul. Because He arrived. He is the Prince of Peace. —SUSANNA FOTH AUGHTMON

FAITH STEP: *What is your chaos this Christmas? Write the Prince of Peace a letter sharing your worries and needs. Invite Him to usher in His peace, hope, and healing to your life today.*

Monday, December 8

Cleanse me with hyssop, and I will be clean; wash me, and I will be whiter than snow.... Create in me a pure heart, O God, and renew a steadfast spirit within me. Psalm 51:7, 10 (NIV)

WHEN I LIVED IN GUATEMALA, I learned all about *la quema del diablo* ("burning of the devil"). Every year, on December 7, the Mayan people clean their homes, sweeping the dirt and refuse into a pile outside their door. When the sun sets, they light the piles on fire. Up and down every street, those fires burn, making it a glorious sight. The indigenous people believe that the flames draw the evil spirits out and into the fire, making their homes both physically and spiritually clean. It's how they prepare for Christmas.

Where I live now, in New Hampshire, our municipality doesn't allow fires on the street. So I've adapted the custom by filling trash bags. As I purge and clean cabinets and closets, I put what is broken or won't serve anyone into the bag for the dump. What is in good shape and could benefit someone else I put in the bag for donation. While I work, I pray for Jesus to bless each space of my home, and to bless each person who will receive the items I pass on. I also ask Him to shine a light on my mistakes so I can repent of my sins, metaphorically sweeping my soul clean too. It's my version of preparing my home and heart for the coming of Christmas.
—CLAIRE MCGARRY

FAITH STEP: *Pick a cabinet or closet to clean out this Advent, praying for Jesus to bless you and the organization you donate to.*

Monday, December 8

> And let the peace that comes from Christ rule in your hearts. For as members of one body you are called to live in peace. And always be thankful. Colossians 3:15 (NLT)

WHEN I WAS TRYING TO drop some pounds before Christmas one year, my friend and amateur fitness guru pushed me a lot: do more reps, add more weight, do more cardio, eat organic. And my husband, who walks a mile more than I can when we work out together, told me I should press through the pain in my muscles and joints. I gave their good advice considerable effort, but in my heart, I had no peace that I could sustain that level of effort long term. The food I was encouraged to consume was often bland and unfulfilling. I was hungry between meals and then unsatisfied when I finally got to eat. As far as exercise, I didn't feel like I could push my body any harder. And the last thing I needed was another six-week weight loss program where I lost pounds only to see most of them return. I still had no solution, and no peace. What was wrong with me?

When I got away from the noise and spent time with Jesus, He answered that question: "Nothing is wrong with you, you just need a plan that's right for *you*." That gave my heart so much peace. In a short time, it became clear that intermittent fasting and moderate but consistent exercise at home was the right plan for me. I followed peace, and I continue to see good results. —PAMELA TOUSSAINT HOWARD

FAITH STEP: *Ask the Holy Spirit for guidance when you have tried and failed to accomplish something. He has a peace-filled plan of success just for you!*

Monday, December 8

I alone know the plans I have for you, plans to bring you prosperity and not disaster, plans to bring about the future you hope for.
Jeremiah 29:11 (GNT)

I AM NOT A FAN of snow. I enjoy watching it float down from above when I'm inside and my fireplace is crackling. To drive or walk in it, praying I won't spin into a ditch? That's no fun.

You might think I'd be used to the icy white fluff after living in Illinois for twenty-five years. But when we moved here from Los Angeles, we had no idea.

One moonlit evening as my husband, Kevin, and I gazed out our picture window to the church parking lot next door, I witnessed a chilling sight. Two cars in the deep snow spinning in circles.

"Honey, call 911," I cried. "Those people are in trouble!"

Kevin told me to look again. It seemed the drivers were doing this snow-dance on purpose. The cars twisted and turned some more then skated down the road and vanished.

The next day I learned that locals call this activity "doing doughnuts," a fun pastime especially for teenagers during the winter months. Who knew?

That experience reminded me how I often look at daunting situations and initially panic based on outward appearances. Once I learn what's happening behind the scenes, I relax.

Jesus knows what He's doing. He's at work in every circumstance, including ones that seem out of control. Jesus is steering my life into a lovely, hope-filled future, even when snow is involved.
—JEANETTE LEVELLIE

FAITH STEP: *Close your eyes and imagine Jesus's hands like the circle of a doughnut, cupped around a situation that needs to change. Ask Jesus to infuse that circumstance with His hope.*

Tuesday, December 9

"But seek first his kingdom and his righteousness, and all these things will be given to you as well." Matthew 6:33 (NIV)

A WEEK BEFORE CHRISTMAS, AND my traditional cleaning frenzy was in full swing. I remembered my mom on her hands and knees, scrubbing the baseboards, polishing every surface. The sponge doesn't fall far from the sink. I had additional pressure to be ready because we were hosting a family birthday party in a few days. How would I ever get it all done?

Moving things so I could polish the counter, I set the new toaster oven on the washer. Leaving the utility room, I heard a crash. The oven, my husband's gift from me, lay on the floor, mangled. Undaunted, I moved to the next catastrophe. Hurriedly removing my cherished musical angel from her box, I broke off a re-glued wing. Dusting the shelf *behind* the Christmas tree, I knocked a precious glass ornament to the unforgiving tile floor.

I fled to the couch, put my head in my hands, and cried out, *Jesus, help me!* No response. I shouldn't have been surprised. Amid all my Christmas preparations, I'd neglected to prepare for Him. And it was *His* birthday!

Then and there, I went to the quiet place where I meet Jesus, gathering my devotional book and Bible in front of me. I read my daily devotion and the Christmas story in Luke. I asked Jesus to forgive me for not prioritizing Him over preparations. I felt Him whisper, *It's OK.*

Things would get done or they wouldn't. What mattered most was my connection to Jesus. —PAT BUTLER DYSON

FAITH STEP: *During the hectic holiday season, promise Jesus you will spend the first minutes of every day with Him, no matter how much you need to do.*

ADVENT DAY 10 MIDDAY

Tuesday, December 9

Now everyone who competes exercises self-control in everything. However, they do it to receive a crown that will fade away, but we a crown that will never fade away. 1 Corinthians 9:25 (HCSB)

"I WAS AN ANIMAL!" SAID my neighbor, as she described her reaction upon hearing she had won second place in our town's annual Christmas decorating contest. She candidly reenacted her indignation upon learning which house won first place: "You've gotta be kidding me! Blow-up decorations? I thought this was a Christmas *decorating* contest!" Her animated portrayal of her outrage was hilarious. I laughed as she regaled me with her comedic confession, emphatically reiterating, "I was *an animal*!"

Hearing her story reminded me how much I dislike competition. But upon further reflection, I realize, in spite of always claiming I'm not competitive, I've not only created and organized contests, I've also competed in more than my fair share of competitions—auditions, games, races, and tournaments. I wouldn't say competition brings out the animal in me, but I've won some prizes. I've also gone home empty-handed.

The Apostle Paul wrote that in a race only one person gets the prize (1 Corinthians 9:24). If that's true, by myself I wouldn't stand a chance. To assure success in collaborative competitions, it helps to be paired with someone highly qualified. Which is why, in this great contest of life, I need to be with Jesus. I'm counting on Him for the win. And to help me with my self-control—so I won't behave like an animal, win or lose. —CASSANDRA TIERSMA

FAITH STEP: *Try a little friendly competition today—rock/paper/scissors, tic-tac-toe, or even a game of solitaire. Before playing the game, thank Jesus for helping you exercise self-control in the contest of life.*

Tuesday, December 9

You must each decide in your heart how much to give. And don't give reluctantly or in response to pressure. "For God loves a person who gives cheerfully." 2 Corinthians 9:7 (NLT)

My older son, Pierce, and I love to share funny memes and reels. Scrolling on social media, I came across a *Saturday Night Live* skit that had me in stitches. Maybe you've seen it. The scene opens on Christmas morning, and everyone is happily opening piles of spectacular packages and stockings brimming with treats, except long-suffering, martyr-mom who gets only one gift—a robe, which was on sale.

Pierce and I laughed out loud. Soon after, though, Pierce said he needed to run out for some unplanned errands. It took me a minute and a few probing questions to understand the skit made him feel bad, and he wanted to get me more gifts. My heart sank. I reassured him that I'd be thrilled with whatever he'd already purchased.

But it wasn't always that way. I spent many martyr years receiving gifts with critical expectations nobody met or even knew about. I gave when I really didn't feel led to or couldn't afford it. My presents sometimes had strings attached, all in a subconscious effort to fill the deficits of my childhood. Longing for love, I'd give gifts desperate for approval or out of duty rather than genuine caring.

Intensive healing work and continually deepening my relationship with Jesus and my understanding of His unconditional love and grace satisfied and reconfigured my heart. Sure, I enjoy presents, but they're not the focus. Even if I open a robe this year, I know Jesus is the real gift. —Isabella Campolattaro

Faith Step: *Are you a cheerful giver? On a gift bag or piece of wrapping paper write the words of 2 Corinthians 9:7. Place it where you can check your heart throughout the season.*

ADVENT DAY 11 MORNING

WEDNESDAY, DECEMBER 10

"Come now, let us settle the matter," says the Lord. "Though your sins are like scarlet, they shall be as white as snow; though they are red as crimson, they shall be like wool." Isaiah 1:18 (NIV)

EVERY YEAR, MY IN-LAWS GIVE us money to buy something special for Christmas. This past December, my husband, Scott, and I decided to invest their generous gift in something extra special and magical—a snow blower!

We've been in Idaho for five years. We experience the joy of living in a winter wonderland where the entire Treasure Valley is blanketed in pristine snow. While I liked shoveling the snow from our driveway, Scott regularly threatened to move back to California. I understand. We get a whole lot of snow! We would both end up with backaches associated with the cleanup. But now with the flip of a switch, this machine does all the heavy lifting. Scott cleared our snowy driveway in record time this past week. This new snowblower is a beautiful thing.

There are a lot of areas in my life where I need help, not just clearing driveways. I struggle with pride and anxiety. I wrestle with doubt and fear. Coveting has been an issue since childhood. (I want all the things. Especially at Christmas!) I can't change my heart or overcome my struggles, but Jesus can (Psalm 51:10). When I confess my weaknesses, Jesus forgives my sins, making me white as snow. He saves me and gives me a new way to live. Jesus does all the heavy lifting. Now that is a beautiful thing. —SUSANNA FOTH AUGHTMON

FAITH STEP: *In what area of life do you need Jesus's help and forgiveness? Talk to Him about it now.*

WEDNESDAY, DECEMBER 10

If it is possible, as far as it depends on you, live at peace with everyone. Romans 12:18 (NIV)

THE PHONE BUZZED, AND I could feel my face flush as I read the text message. The news didn't surprise me, yet I was still irritated at the last-minute cancellation. "Thanks a lot for the heads-up, shows how little you value spending time with the family," I furiously tapped out, and showed it to my husband. "Should you send that?" he gently questioned.

I struggle to tame my tongue (and my fingers), but something about the holidays and family gatherings tests my willpower. As I continued to type, the words I tell my children flashed into my mind: You can't control your circumstances, but you can control your response.

I realize it's not always possible to live at peace. Sometimes I must speak up, which may rock the boat, hurt feelings, or cause discord. But this text wasn't that. I deleted my reply, choosing not to allow my hurt feelings to cause tension in our relationship. I asked the Holy Spirit to guide my words and examine my heart. "Thanks for letting me know. Merry Christmas," I typed, before I could change my mind, and hit send. When I laid my head down that night, I could say I had done my part to keep peace on earth, and in my relationship with my family. —LAURA BAILEY

FAITH STEP: *Take a moment and scroll through your texts. Are you sending the peace of Jesus with the words you type?*

ADVENT DAY 11 EVENING

WEDNESDAY, DECEMBER 10

The Word became a human being and, full of grace and truth, lived among us. John 1:14 (GNT)

"This year, I just want a simple meal for Christmas. Meat, potatoes, veggies, and dessert," I told my husband, Kevin. "I don't want to cook and clean up for hours."

Kevin agreed that Jesus's birthday was for honoring Him and enjoying family. He said he'd grill steaks, I could pop in some potatoes, and the kids could bring the rest. Simple.

But for some peculiar reason, the baked potatoes turned into our daughter's favorite potato dish, which required extra shopping and prep. Someone (it might have been me) added a green bean casserole in addition to the bowl of plain corn. And sweet Hawaiian rolls miraculously appeared on the table right before dinner.

We enjoyed a lovely meal. But not a simple one. My penchant for wanting every experience to feel huge and significant took over the wisdom of our marvelous plan.

So unlike the plan for Jesus's birth.

Mary, the girl God chose to mother Jesus, was a humble teenager. Her husband, Joseph, worked as a carpenter. And baby Jesus was born in a barn. His crib was a feeding trough.

I believe God planned it that way on purpose so we common, everyday folk could relate to Jesus better. I have no trouble believing that Jesus was divine. But I sometimes wonder if He gets how I feel. Then I remember the event of His birth and life on earth. Yes, He gets me. Even when I complicate His birthday dinner. —JEANETTE LEVELLIE

FAITH STEP: *Search images online to see what a stable looked like in Judea at the time Jesus was born. Thank Him for being fully human, as well as fully divine.*

Thursday, December 11

> "And she will bring forth a Son, and you shall call His name JESUS, for He will save His people from their sins." Matthew 1:21 (NKJV)

I'VE BEEN MEETING WITH A wonderful Christian therapist on Zoom. When I began speaking with her, I had been going through an emotional rough patch. She was instrumental in helping me restore my mental health.

After the crisis passed, we continued our therapeutic journey together. It was then that something else was unearthed. My therapist encouraged me to pray about the issue. She felt there was a "spirit of disappointment" lingering in my life, and she discerned that this might be the cause of several issues that I had spoken about. She was right. Recently, there had been a string of promising work projects that hadn't materialized, I was short on funds for some planned expenses, and several of my friendships had become strained. I felt deeply disappointed.

I prayed and asked Jesus for insight. Meanwhile, I looked back at my life and saw the many hurts that I had experienced—hurts I always thought I had gotten over. But He revealed that I hadn't. Moreover, I'd never forgiven myself for my part in these situations.

Trusting Jesus to complete the healing, I used my quiet time to pray simple prayers of release from any agreement I may have made, consciously or not, with the "spirit of disappointment." I asked for and received His forgiveness and restoration.
—Pamela Toussaint Howard

FAITH STEP: *During this season of the celebration of His birth, dedicate your prayers to asking Jesus to reveal any sinful tendencies or negative attitudes that may linger in your life, and open your heart to receive His healing.*

Thursday, December 11

Do not run until your feet are bare and your throat is dry. But you said, "It's no use! I love foreign gods, and I must go after them." Jeremiah 2:25 (NIV)

WHEN I OPENED THE STORAGE bin, my heart sank. In my exhaustion and rush to pack up Christmas last year, I'd shoved umpteen strands of lights into the bin without winding them up properly. It was the last day of Thanksgiving break now. We had only an hour to decorate the tree before my boys had to go back to college. We'd spend most of that hour untangling that heap of lights.

I've had Advents where my heart has felt like that mess of lights, tangled up and burnt out by holiday expectations: madly searching for the ideal gifts, decorating everything in sight, cramming in celebration after celebration, all because I thought the path to a perfect Christmas was paved with excess. That mindset had me running toward the wrong things, striving to create Christmas rather than receive it.

Now I know it's about the hush not the rush. If I had slowed down last year, I would have avoided burnout by remaining open to what the season brings. Advent peace would have kept my heart untangled and energized, if only I'd taken the time to embrace it.

This year I *will* trim back the excess and stop racing past what truly matters. It's the slow pace of Advent that's lined with gifts, ones that are best received with empty hands and an open heart.
—CLAIRE MCGARRY

FAITH STEP: *Find a quiet spot and sit with your palms opened toward heaven. Close your eyes and whisper Jesus's name. Feel His peace in the hush.*

Thursday, December 11

Love is patient, love is kind. It does not envy, it does not boast, it is not proud. 1 Corinthians 13:4 (NIV)

THE PEANUT BLOSSOM COOKIES I make at Christmas are famous, at least in my family. So when my daughter Melissa asked to make them for our family Christmas Eve gathering, I was horrified. Those were *my* signature cookies. I couldn't turn them over to a woman who burns toast.

"Those cookies are harder to make than they look," I told Melissa. "And six dozen takes a long time."

But Melissa wouldn't be dissuaded. With a jealous heart, I turned over the recipe and the ingredients I'd assembled. I couldn't resist calling her with some helpful tips. "Fold the flour into the creamed mixture rather than using a mixer." She didn't know what "fold" meant. "Refrigerate the dough for an hour to make it easier to work with." She hung up quickly.

Since I didn't have cookies to bake, I collapsed on the sofa. *Jesus, what's wrong with me? It's just cookies! Why am I so upset?*

I heard Him whisper, *Pride, Pat. Beware.*

That night when we gathered at my son's house, Melissa came in bearing a large grocery bag. "Where are the cookies?" I asked.

"Oh, Mom, we made such a mess of them, but we had fun! I bought cupcakes! With sprinkles! Love you, Mama!" *Store-bought cupcakes?* Everyone else seemed excited about them. Did anyone ask about my peanut blossoms? Nope. I swallowed my pride and had a cupcake. —PAT BUTLER DYSON

FAITH STEP: *Ask Jesus to help you examine your heart and rein in your pride.*

Friday, December 12

The whole earth is at rest and quiet; they break forth into singing.
Isaiah 14:7 (ESV)

IT WAS EERILY STILL AND quiet as my daughter and I drove miles along the ordinarily busy seven-lane thoroughfare in the city. Ours was the only car on the road. Not a single business was open. Evidently, the world had come to a stop. Due to a last-minute unexpected turn of events, that Christmas Day my daughter and I were, uncharacteristically, home alone. Always up for a spontaneous mother-daughter fun adventure, we decided to go out to eat. In the frigid cold, we found the only open business was a diner at the edge of town, where we ordered warm bowls of soup.

Although a low-key, subdued way to spend Christmas Day, it was, at the same time, exciting and awe-inspiring to witness how celebrating the birth of the Savior impacted the entire population. The normally bustling commercial world we live in was at a standstill in recognition of Jesus's birthday. From devout followers of Christ to ardent disbelievers, all were of one accord, their doors closed to commemorate the most miraculous birth in the history of the world. The birth of Jesus, the Son of God.

This Advent season, I want to savor the awe of that realization. Amidst the usual Advent and Christmas activities this year, I'm treasuring the memory of a Christmas when the world stood still in honor of Jesus's birth. —CASSANDRA TIERSMA

FAITH STEP: *Whether alone or with others, enjoy a bowl of soup and reflect on the awe-inspiring fact that Jesus, born more than two thousand years ago, is still impacting the world today.*

Friday, December 12

> *"Where, O death, is your victory? Where, O death, is your sting?"*
> 1 Corinthians 15:55 (NIV)

That Christmas Eve, tears formed in my eyes. Tipping my candle, I watched the flame catch the wick. The sanctuary lights dimmed and the first notes of "Silent Night" flowed from the organ.

Memories flooded my thoughts. "Silent Night" had been my son, Steven's, favorite song. As a boy, he asked me to sing it to him at bedtime. I watched the flame dance while the congregation sang. Ever since my son had been killed in a car crash, "Silent Night" affected me deeply. My loss overshadowed Mary's faith and Jesus's miraculous birth.

As the flame flickered, I had a feeling that the light was trying to tell me something. I could almost hear Jesus saying, "I am the light." I thought about Mary. We had both lost our sons. How much worse it must have been for her. The anguish she must have lived through. My mother's heart burst in sorrow for Mary.

Knowing my son was in heaven with her Son eased my pain. Jesus was holding Steven now. I felt a deep connection to Mary.

As the congregation sang "Silent Night," I took solace in the words. I held my candle tighter and softly sang the last verse: "sleep in heavenly peace." —Jeannie Hughes

Faith Step: *Do you feel pain from the loss of a loved one? Believe in Jesus's promise that they are with Him in heaven.*

Friday, December 12

> *Look to the LORD and his strength; seek his face always.*
> 1 Chronicles 16:11 (NIV)

TYPICALLY, I ENTER THE HOLIDAY season with anticipation. I'm usually energized by feelings of hope and renewal to celebrate Christ's birth. But this year, I was feeling glum for several reasons. I was rehabbing my knee post-fracture and unable to country line dance with my husband during our monthly get-together with pals. I missed my oldest daughter, who was away on a winter vacation with friends. Two of my favorite radio programs were canceled, disrupting my nightly routine. Bored and melancholy, I retreated to my room to write in my journal.

Opening the cover, I skimmed last year's goals, which I had written on the first page, and one stood out as incomplete: *Spend more time not only in Scripture but in prayer.* I didn't recall making that one. I had to admit I'd failed to devote the time.

Jesus always found time to pray. Prayer allowed Him to praise (Matthew 11:25), to recharge (Mark 1:35), to petition (John 17:1). Maybe I was feeling pensive this year because I was focused on my losses, not my blessings. I needed to focus on Jesus. My busy calendar cleared, it was time to fold my hands and seek Him. —GLORIA JOYCE

FAITH STEP: *Find a quiet moment to read Scripture and pray. Then imagine the face of Jesus. Feel His presence, love, and acceptance.*

Saturday, December 13

For we walk by faith, not by sight. 2 Corinthians 5:7 (NKJV)

As a girl growing up in the Upper Peninsula of Michigan, I always experienced white Christmases. There was never a question in my mind as to whether or not we'd have snow because we always did. One year, when I was about twelve years old, my dad, mom, brother, and I spent Christmas in Florida visiting my uncle and his family. The weather was bright and sunny with palm trees swaying in the warm breeze. I remember feeling sad because it was eighty-something degrees. Nothing about the day felt like Christmas at all.

Years passed and I grew up. I have since married and now live in Georgia where most Christmases are not white. It still feels odd to me going through the holiday season being able to see sidewalks instead of snowmen. But because I've had the opportunity to live in these different places, Jesus has helped me see that Christmas isn't dependent upon my environment. Christmas is a celebration. More than that, it's a celebration about what I can't see, not what I can.

I wasn't there all those years ago to witness the miraculous birth of Jesus. I wasn't there to see Mary lay Him in that manger or hear His first sweet cries. Still I choose to believe the incredible story, passed down from generation to generation, of our Savior's birth.

The truth is, I never needed snow to celebrate Christmas. I just needed a faith-filled heart. —Kristen West

---

Faith Step: *Do you feel like it's just not Christmas because there's something missing in your environment? Take a moment, look inward, and ponder the condition of your heart.*

SATURDAY, DECEMBER 13

And they went with haste and found Mary and Joseph, and the baby lying in a manger. Luke 2:16 (ESV)

"Drat!" I said as another cookie stuck to my rolling pin. It was almost Christmas, and I was trying to make sugar cookies for my family to decorate. When I was growing up, my mother would make her own sugar cookies and frosting, and together we would decorate them on Christmas Eve. Now that my own kids were old enough to help decorate, I was determined to keep the tradition alive.

But nothing was working! Every time I tried to roll out the cookie dough, it stuck to the counter and the pin. Before I could place the stars on the cookie sheet, they fell apart in my hands. Tears streamed down my cheeks. "Nothing is going right!" I wailed.

"Hey," my husband said, "what's happening in here?"

"I can't get these cookies to hold their shape," I wailed.

"Why do they have to be stars?" he asked. "Blobs taste good too!" We both laughed.

"Let's cool down a minute." He made me a cup of tea. "You think you're having a hard time, but imagine how Mary felt."

I paused, smiled, then sat at the kitchen table and sipped my cup. Here I was trying to make perfect cookies for Christmas, but now I was reminded that nothing was perfect when Jesus was born. An unwed mother, no room at the inn, and strange shepherds crowding around a baby in a manger.

On Christmas Eve, as my family gathered to decorate our Christmas blobs, I pondered the miracle of Jesus's birth and took a bite of a cookie. Our imperfect creations were perfectly delicious! As witnessed by Jesus's life on earth, imperfect beginnings can result in profoundly perfect results. —Heather Jepsen

Faith Step: *Take a break and have a snack as you ponder all the seemingly imperfect events surrounding Jesus's birth.*

SATURDAY, DECEMBER 13

You will keep him in perfect peace, whose mind is stayed on You, because he trusts in You. Isaiah 26:3 (NKJV)

CHRISTMAS IS COMING—AND FAST. EVERYWHERE I turn, people rush about, seemingly frantic to get things done in time. Gift lists and checkout lines are long. Many friends and loved ones to remember, lots of gifts to wrap. Carols blare in every shop and from every radio station, until I can't wait for January. Bright colored lights outline homes and circle trees, fun to put up but hard to take down. The scents of fresh-baked goodies fill the air, eggnog fills my mouth and belly, and I avoid the bathroom scale. My senses are on overload, my nerves are frayed, and I'm exhausted.

Sometimes I wonder what God thinks about the way we celebrate Jesus's birth. All the hoopla, distractions, and overindulgences. But then I remember, we are His children, imperfect yet loved. I believe God's not surprised when we gum things up or behave outside the realm of perfection. It's expected. After all, we're sinners and still learning. I believe His desire for us is to acknowledge and celebrate the Savior's role in our lives, and reap the peace that comes solely from Him. A peace that flows smoothly and never stops, that enters and fills us, even when we run out of gift wrap or burn the cookies. Especially during those times. —HEIDI GAUL

FAITH STEP: *Write the words of Isaiah 26:3 on a notecard and memorize them. When something goes wrong during this holiday season, whisper the verse until peace finds you.*

JOY

Joy to the world; the Lord is come;
Let Earth receive her King;
Let ev'ry heart prepare him room,
And heav'n and nature sing.

Joy to the Earth, the Savior reigns;
Our mortal songs employ,
While fields and floods, rocks, hills and plains,
Repeat the sounding joy.

Third Sunday of Advent, December 14

Shout for joy to the LORD, all the earth. Worship the LORD with gladness; come before him with joyful songs. Psalm 100:1–2 (NIV)

As I walked through the main doors for the Christmas vigil service, I recognized that my heart wasn't in it. I preferred to attend services on Christmas Day, but this year's change in plans made it impossible.

Glowing trees and plump poinsettias decorated the solemn scene. Parents, grandparents, and children alike were reverently dressed for the celebration of Jesus's birth. As the choir finished singing "The Gloria" and the ringing bells ceased their reverberation, a child's voice from a rear pew caught everyone's attention. "Yea!" The boy's innocent glee elicited chuckles from the congregation and his parents, even as they tried to keep him quiet. After each song the choir sang, the child repeated the same cry of joy. Still grumpy, I sat with my arms folded.

A little while later, when he gave his homily, our pastor, Father Janton, commented on the joy that had sprung from our young parishioner. Then following the distribution of Communion, Father Janton shared his own joy over Christ's birth when he spontaneously stepped over to the cantor's microphone and belted out an acapella rendition of "How Great Thou Art," which further jostled me out of my sullenness. An eruption of applause echoed from the congregation, and I joined in the ovation, suddenly feeling guilty for grumbling about my upset plans. Had I not been there, I would have missed an inspiring outpouring of joy from a child during a special celebration of the birth of another. —Gloria Joyce

Faith Step: *If you find your plans altered today, be flexible and watch for the unexpected blessing from Jesus.*

Third Sunday of Advent, December 14

Yes, the LORD has done amazing things for us! What joy! Psalm 126:3 (NLT)

OUR ROWDY FAMILY HUSHED AS my husband, Jeff, announced, "I want y'all to come take a look at my new ride." Of the fifteen of us, only my grandson Ty was clueless as to what would happen next.

Four years earlier, Ty had gotten sick with a mysterious illness that left him homebound. How I'd prayed for doctors to find an answer and cure. Two years passed, then three, and I continued to pray for a breakthrough. By the fourth year, our now sixteen-year-old grandson had become more isolated, and I wondered if Jesus was listening.

On the driveway, I shivered with anticipation, as Jeff backed out a shiny black pickup truck with a huge red ribbon spread across the hood. "Ty, Ty, Ty!" we shouted.

The look on my grandson's face was pure ecstasy! I glanced around and saw that joy mirrored on the faces of Ty's parents and grandparents, aunts, uncles, and cousins. Everyone had prayed for Ty, and this new pickup represented a new start.

Ty climbed into the driver's seat of his pickup truck, grinning like his old self. I felt confident he would learn to drive, reconnect with friends from school, and go places. His life would improve. Thank You, Jesus! —PAT BUTLER DYSON

FAITH STEP: *When in your life were you most joyful? Pray for Jesus to inspire you on how to amaze someone with an extra special gift or action at Christmas.*

Third Sunday of Advent, December 14

Though he was God, he did not think of equality with God as something to cling to. Instead, he gave up his divine privileges; he took the humble position of a slave and was born as a human being. Philippians 2:6–7 (NLT)

Our three cats are in-and-out beings. Pokey stays in, except when the sun is warm. Wally is in and out most of the day and early evening. And Princess Di would live outside if she didn't need food and cuddles.

Two weeks ago on a frigid day, I called Princess to come in. She sat stiff and regal on a throne of snow, just staring at me. After I coaxed her inside with the promise of a second breakfast, she finally relented and left her snowy seat.

As God from eternity, Jesus reigned supreme in heaven. But at the appointed time set by the Father, Jesus stepped down from His throne, set His royal garments aside, and strode into time and humanity.

Jesus never debated whether He would stay in heaven to rule the universe or come to earth and live as a man. His love for us was that great. He said yes to the perfect plan to save us and bring us into His family.

Unlike my foolish cat who found joy on her icy throne, Jesus found His deepest joy in leaving His royal throne for us. And that is Christmas. —Jeanette Levellie

Faith Step: *Sit on a chair with a cape or jacket around your shoulders. Close your eyes and imagine yourself in a lavish castle with thousands of servants at your command. Now take the cape off, open your eyes, look up, and say yes to God's plan for you.*

ADVENT DAY 16 MORNING

MONDAY, DECEMBER 15

Therefore, as God's chosen people, holy and dearly loved, clothe yourselves with compassion, kindness, humility, gentleness and patience. Colossians 3:12 (NIV)

THE HOLIDAY SERMON BEGAN WITH a simple question: Are you a thermometer or a thermostat? The pastor held my full attention.

"A thermometer reacts to the temperature in the room. It assesses the situation and records the number. If it's sixty-eight degrees, the thermometer reads sixty-eight. What happens in the room controls the thermometer."

I wondered where his illustration was headed and how it could be related to Christmas.

"A thermostat sets the room temperature. It assesses the situation and takes action. If it's sixty-eight degrees and it's supposed to be seventy, the thermostat causes the heating unit to start. The thermostat controls what happens in the room."

Skillfully, the pastor morphed the story about furnace parts into a cheerful challenge for listeners: At Christmas gatherings, don't react—take action to add Christlike attributes to the atmosphere. I thought of the fruit of the Spirit in relation to my own upcoming celebrations. Most were sure to possess compassion, kindness, and humility. But one event on my calendar had the potential to be lacking in gentleness and patience. I pondered how I might be a thermostat that day. Perhaps I could change the temperature in the room to a holly jolly level that honors Jesus. —BECKY ALEXANDER

FAITH STEP: *Prepare for an upcoming gathering by listing the fruit of the Spirit on a piece of paper. Place it near a thermostat in your home as a reminder.*

Monday, December 15

> *"Do not store up for yourselves treasures on earth, where moths and vermin destroy, and where thieves break in and steal. But store up for yourselves treasures in heaven.... For where your treasure is, there your heart will be also."* Matthew 6:19–21 (NIV)

My parents were Italian, and we sometimes spent Christmas in Italy when I was little, an altogether different experience than our American celebration, especially way back then. I vividly remember one Christmas, I was around eight, when we visited my maternal grandparents in Naples. My Nonno Rodolfo was a prosperous banker, and they lived in a spacious apartment in an elegant building at a swanky address.

Yet notwithstanding their affluence, I received only one gift, but I was positively thrilled. It was a toy nursing kit, complete with nurse's costume, bonnet, stethoscope, and assorted other medical essentials for pretending. I can still recall my wide-eyed delight when I opened it. The fact that it was just one thoughtful gift made it even more precious. The focus of the holiday was the meals and reverentially honoring the Nativity story at Catholic mass. Contrast that with the dozens of gifts I give to my children today—many forgotten in days or weeks at best.

Jesus's words remind us of what really matters, inviting us to store up heartfelt spiritual treasures that will outlast the piles of stuff we'll leave behind. Jesus, the fulfillment of all things (Ephesians 1:23), the satisfaction of our soul's longing (Psalm 107:9), entirely sufficient (2 Corinthians 12:9), wrapped in swaddling clothes and love, is the lasting gift I most want to share with my children.
—Isabella Campolattaro

Faith Step: *Consider talking with your family about scaling down Christmas gifts this year, perhaps even dramatically.*

Monday, December 15

For by grace you have been saved through faith, and that not of yourselves; it is the gift of God. Ephesians 2:8 (NKJV)

EVERY YEAR DURING THE HOLIDAYS, my brother Rick posts a special photo on social media, one that brings a smile to my face. It's a circa 1960s black-and-white portrait of the three of us—my sister Joanna, Rick, and me—with Santa. Joanna is seated in a ladylike pose on one side and Rick on the other, his face radiating unadulterated joy. I stand between them with Santa sitting behind me, his hands resting lightly on my shoulders. My small hands grasp a cellophane-wrapped candy cane as if it were spun gold, my expression one of sheer bliss with a sprinkling of awe. It's no wonder, really. I've just asked a seemingly all-powerful person to fulfill my dreams. Toys, dolls, whatever my heart wished for, I'd entrusted this man to deliver. After all, I'd been good.

Needless to say, I don't believe in Santa anymore. Instead, I place my trust in the One who provides for all my needs, and many of my wants. Jesus. It's Him I live for now, and He alone I strive to please. As I stand before Him daily, I sense His acceptance and approval. I can almost feel His hands on my shoulders, guiding me. I have no need of candy canes or empty promises. For in my heart, I hold tightly to the greatest gift ever given: Jesus, and the grace that flows through Him. —HEIDI GAUL

FAITH STEP: *For today and every day this week, imagine you are posing for a Christmas photo with Jesus. Does your face reflect the joy and awe of accepting His great gift?*

Tuesday, December 16

> *Shout for joy to the Lord, all the earth, burst into jubilant song with music; make music to the Lord with the harp, with the harp and the sound of singing, with trumpets and the blast of the ram's horn—shout for joy before the Lord, the King.* Psalm 98:4–6 (NIV)

WHEN MY HUSBAND, JASON, AND I went to Israel for a mission trip, we came home with a shofar—a Jewish musical instrument typically made from a ram's horn that is used in religious ceremonies or blown to signify important occasions. The following Christmas, Jason thought it would be a great idea to use the shofar to wake the kids on Christmas morning. The problem was that we didn't realize how difficult it would be to use. Instead of a strong, commanding call to attention, it sounded more like a sad little balloon losing its air. Our kids awoke to our laughter rather than the blast of a ram's horn.

Though Jason has never learned how to properly blow the shofar, he still tries every Christmas morning. Just the presence of the shofar makes the day seem special, even if we have to imagine the proper sounds. In the Bible, a ram's horn is used for many reasons. It's a call to prayer (1 Chronicles 16:39-42). It cries out in battle (Joshua 6:20). It also signifies the anointing of a king (1 Kings 1:39), which makes it the perfect addition to our holiday traditions. Jesus is our King of kings, and we love celebrating His birth with the sounding of a shofar—even if our attempts do result in hilarity. —EMILY E. RYAN

FAITH STEP: *Look up videos of someone blowing a shofar. Consider how you might incorporate one into your Christmas celebration.*

ADVENT DAY 17 MIDDAY

TUESDAY, DECEMBER 16

There is a time for everything, and a season for every activity under the heavens. Ecclesiastes 3:1 (NIV)

OUR SON IS A YOUNG adult, so these days, Christmas starts midmorning. I get up just early enough to make my husband and son's favorite French toast brunch. Before our first bite, we pause to give thanks for Jesus's birth. Later, we'll head out for our newish Christmas movie-night tradition. Long gone are those early Christmas mornings when our son shook us awake and met our eyes with his wide-toothed smile, excited for what he might find under the tree.

When I was a kid, one of my favorite things about Christmas (besides getting gifts) was being in pajamas as long as possible that day. My family always did it—even after my sister married—and I couldn't wait to experience this pajama-tradition with my husband on our first Christmas. He was hesitant, but I convinced him that it was tradition. So he agreed, and we arrived at my parents' home only to find everyone fully dressed in regular clothes. Apparently, those pajama days were gone.

Christmas has changed through the years and familiar routines have been replaced with new realities. Sometimes the day is filled with driving long hours, exchanging gifts, and reconnecting with family; other times the day is quiet and relaxing, at home with my husband and son. What has remained the same each Christmas is the love and joy Jesus brings wherever and however we celebrate His birth. —ERICKA LOYNES

FAITH STEP: *Take a moment and look at Christmas photos. Bask in the love and joy you felt when those pictures were taken.*

TUESDAY, DECEMBER 16

Let us therefore come boldly unto the throne of grace, that we may obtain mercy, and find grace to help in time of need. Hebrews 4:16 (KJV)

I HAVE ALWAYS LOVED THE Christmas season: celebrating Jesus's birth, the way the daylight begins to increase, the freshness of being on the verge of a new year, my family, yummy food, and our special traditions. One thing has changed though. My wedding anniversary was during that time and now I no longer celebrate it.

With the end of my thirty-year marriage, I have found growing freedom, joy, and physical and mental health. But it also cost dearly. The gift of those things came wrapped up in a lot of pain, confusion, suffering, and shame. It has been a process to embrace the gifts and shed the wrapping. I spend a lot of time at the foot of the Cross, leaving the heartache there time and again, exchanging fear and sorrow for mercy and grace. Letting Jesus lift my head. Accepting the love and strength He holds out to me in His nail-scarred hands.

Jesus entered the world as a human to understand us in our hunger, our fear, our filth, our isolation. That's what His birth to the teenaged Mary in a lowly Bethlehem stable meant. He gave His life to fill us with a love so strong and secure that we could approach God with boldness, knowing our worth. Confident we can trust Him. Sure that we belong. —GWEN FORD FAULKENBERRY

FAITH STEP: *What does God hold out to you that you're afraid to receive? His love, joy, peace? Hope for the future? Stand up, step forward, and grasp it. It's yours.*

ADVENT DAY 18 MORNING

WEDNESDAY, DECEMBER 17

But the angel said to them, "Do not be afraid. I bring you good news that will cause great joy for all the people. Today in the town of David a Savior has been born to you; he is the Messiah, the Lord." Luke 2:10–11 (NIV)

I TAUGHT FOUR-YEAR-OLD SADIE ABOUT Jesus with intentionality—every time we were together. Occasionally she'd say, "You've already told me that, Grammy." I'd reply, "That's OK. I'm going to tell you again." The holiday season especially provided teachable moments, and I took advantage of them all.

"We're supposed to share the good news of Christmas with other people," I said. "Do you know what the good news is?"

"I'm not sure. What is it?" Sadie asked.

"Jesus came to the earth as a baby."

With perfect comedic timing, she quipped, "Well, what's the bad news?"

After a big laugh, I felt a sense of great joy rising inside of me. Because of the gift of Jesus's birth, I could give my granddaughter a glorious answer—there is no bad news! All the news is good. Forgiveness from sins (Matthew 1:21). Abundant life on earth (John 10:10). An eternal home in heaven (John 14:2). The list goes on and on.

The world wants Sadie to think good news is always accompanied by something bad. I even fall into that frame of mind at times. A happy day, followed by a hard day. A success, then a failure. But Jesus wants both of us to know He is the exception. And He used a funny question from a four-year-old to teach me that truth.

—BECKY ALEXANDER

FAITH STEP: *Make a "Good News List" with red and green pens. Name blessings brought to you by the birth of Jesus. Read them aloud in a prayer of thanks.*

WEDNESDAY, DECEMBER 17

> Remember to do good and help each other. Gifts like this please God.
> —Hebrews 13:16 (NLV)

DRAGGING IN AFTER CHRISTMAS SHOPPING, I felt empty and downhearted. I'd spent too much money and wasn't even sure the recipients would appreciate my gifts. *It feels like Christmas is too much about gifts, Jesus. Show me some way to make Christmas meaningful this year.*

Jesus got right to work. My friend Deanna, a counselor who works with nursing home patients, called me later that day. She does group therapy with the patients, helping them develop coping skills. In addition, her patients do crafts, paint, play bingo and tossing games. They celebrate every holiday with gifts and treats.

"We're running low on snacks," Deanna said. "Could you provide some?" I jumped at the chance. "Also puzzles, lip balm, and socks. Socks are favorite bingo prizes."

Deanna sent me a link and I ordered treats online—chips, cookies, candy bars, popcorn, along with puzzles, lip balm, and lots of socks. It took so little time. I didn't give it another thought.

Several days after Christmas, I received a thank-you card I'll always treasure. Thirty-two nursing home residents had signed it—Gaylene, Rodney, Jarvis. Wanita, Paul, and Arisha, to name a few. Those precious signatures, some shakier than others, touched my heart. This had been such a small thing, requiring so little of my time and money, but it was the most satisfying of gifts. It made Christmas especially meaningful, not only for the nursing home recipients but for me. —PAT BUTLER DYSON

FAITH STEP: *Stop by a nursing home or care center and offer to bring snacks or provide small gifts.*

WEDNESDAY, DECEMBER 17

"I am the good shepherd. The good shepherd lays down his life for the sheep. The hired hand is not the shepherd and does not own the sheep." John 10:11–12 (NIV)

THE OTHER NIGHT MY HUSBAND and I were watching television. I can't recall the program, but there was a teenager in a T-shirt with the Esprit logo, popular back in the eighties.

My husband asked if I wore Esprit in those days.

"Nope," I said. Designer brands tended to exceed my clothing allowance back then.

"Did you have the off-brand?" he asked. "Did your shirt say 'Spirit'?"

"Yep." I grinned and then we burst out laughing. He understood wardrobe frugality growing up, because he wore mostly hand-me-downs. (Love a good hand-me-down.)

It's been decades since I've thought about either brand—the authentic I wished for and the knockoff that left me a little disappointed.

I'm so glad Jesus never sends a knockoff in His place. Every moment of every day, He is present to hear and care for me—with His authentic Spirit, no less! He never sends a substitute in His place.

Anything but Jesus leaves me wishing and wanting, not only in this Advent season when there's so much focus on gift giving and receiving. How much more I love my authentic Savior who came to give His life for me. —ERIN KEELEY MARSHALL

FAITH STEP: *Look around your house for a knockoff or store brand item that you enjoy. Donate it to a local thrift or ministry shop, and pray that its next owner will experience Jesus as the real deal.*

THURSDAY, DECEMBER 18

> He says to the snow, "Fall on the earth," and to the rain shower, "Be a mighty downpour." —Job 37:6 (NIV)

WHERE I LIVE NEAR HOUSTON, Texas, the Christmas season is seldom described as a winter wonderland. I've spent plenty of Christmas mornings in a T-shirt and shorts, dabbing the sweat from my brow as the southern sun melts away any hint of the winters we see portrayed in holiday movies. As a child, I dreamed of experiencing a white Christmas, but I seldom expected it to actually happen.

However, one Christmas many years ago before I had children, it finally did. As my husband and I walked out of church from the Christmas Eve service, we were surprised to find flurries of snow just beginning to fall and collect on sidewalks and parked cars. The drive home felt like an experience in outer space, with snow flying past us like stars traveling at warp speed. We were giddy with excitement and spent the evening playing in our front yard and catching snowflakes on our tongues. Christmas morning was covered in a blanket of white, a dream come true, and I'll never forget driving on the freeway and seeing the most Texan sight ever: a driver carrying a full-sized snowman in the back of his pickup truck.

I may never experience a white Christmas again, but I'm thankful for the memory. I'm also thankful for Christmases that were hot, rainy, humid, or icy because no matter the weather, the presence of Jesus is the true source of beauty and wonder. —EMILY E. RYAN

FAITH STEP: *As you check the forecast for Christmas Day, thank Jesus for His power over the weather and His presence in every atmospheric condition.*

Thursday, December 18

> *This is the confidence we have in approaching God: that if we ask anything according to his will, he hears us. And if we know that he hears us—whatever we ask—we know that we have what we asked of him.* 1 John 5:14–15 (NIV)

ONE OF THE MANY JOYS of Isaac, my son with Down syndrome, is his perpetual childlike faith. He still believes in Santa Claus, in a matter-of-fact way. While we don't focus on Santa at our house, we do enjoy and indulge Isaac's delight.

To prolong the pleasure—and admittedly simplify life—we have a novel way of creating our Christmas list. Sometime in the fall or winter, I take Isaac to a supercenter, and we stroll the toy aisles. Isaac points out what he likes, and Mommy takes a picture to text to "Santa," who returns later to shop.

This thoroughly modern approach is efficient and fun. It also gives me a chance to fact-check his desires. Sometimes Isaac will pick something he already has and never plays with. Other times, he'll choose an item I really don't want him to have because it's too violent, isn't age-appropriate, is lousy quality, or is too costly.

Often, we discuss inappropriate choices while shopping. I might explain my reasoning for denying him and he'll argue or beg, but I'm unshaken.

I believe our Lord operates the same way when I ask for something—gift, job, outcome, relationship. Being denied what I want is disappointing, but like Isaac, I have faith. I trust Jesus's judgment is perfect, fair, and truly best for me. —ISABELLA CAMPOLATTARO

FAITH STEP: *Ask Jesus to give you His perspective on something you wanted and prayed for but didn't get. Journal what He reveals.*

Thursday, December 18

> *The LORD knows all human plans; he knows that they are futile... For the LORD will not reject his people; he will never forsake his inheritance.* Psalm 94:11, 14 (NIV)

I'VE NOTICED A STEADY DECLINE of holiday mail over the years. I admit that we don't send Christmas cards or letters anymore, but last year, only 10 cards arrived to grace my mantel. Even though digital holiday messages are today's norm, I was still surprised by how light my mailbox was on season's greetings. Several cards and updates I was used to getting never came. It's not so easy for me to accept when seasons of life change, especially when that change results in losing personal connections.

To be honest, I've never been great at staying in touch through letters and phone calls. When I was a young wife and stay-at-home mom, it was certainly fun to try. One year, our Christmas card featured a professional photo. Thrilled with the final design, I doubled the order. In trying to craft the perfect family update, I let time slip away and never mailed those cards—and I haven't mailed one since.

It's good for me to remember that Christmas cards don't accurately represent all the connections I'm blessed to have in my life. I'm grateful for family and friends who initiate contact even when they haven't heard from me in a while. I am even more grateful that when I sometimes fall short of being in touch with Jesus, my most important connection, He never loses contact with me.
—ERICKA LOYNES

FAITH STEP: *Write a letter or a paragraph on a Christmas card to Jesus. Put it somewhere to remind you to stay in contact with Him this holiday season.*

ADVENT DAY 20 MORNING

FRIDAY, DECEMBER 19

And let us run with perseverance the race marked out for us, fixing our eyes on Jesus, the pioneer and perfecter of faith. For the joy set before him he endured the cross, scorning its shame, and sat down at the right hand of the throne of God. Hebrews 12:1–2 (NIV)

THIS CHRISTMASTIME, I'VE GIFTED MYSELF a compact joy spreader that requires no batteries or special equipment to radiate glee: our poochon (poodle/bichon frise mix) puppy, Nugget. He bounds through each morning as only a two-pound bundle of wonder and innocence can. But the simple wisdom he shares is priceless. Like, when things look dark, grab a toy, because there's always a blessing within reach. Or play as long as you can and rest when you must. And my favorite: always stay focused on your provider.

Nugget's eyes brim in anticipation of a grand day, every day, and his bright enthusiasm is contagious. But his delight is only a flash in comparison to the light of eternal satisfaction, the endless bliss found in Jesus. He's the creator of every blessing, the true source of rest for my soul, and the One I stay my thoughts on.

During this season, my mind fills with thoughts of baby Jesus, that perfect image where humanity and divinity meet. This bright-eyed infant would someday bring my broken world blessings of peace and hope. He'd lend purpose to my work and meaning to my times of rest. Jesus alone provides me with the security of knowing I'm watched over, protected, and loved. When He calls I listen and smile. He is joy. And through Him, so am I. —HEIDI GAUL

FAITH STEP: *Do something today to spread the joy of Jesus. Smile. Point out simple blessings. Rest in prayer.*

Friday, December 19

"I have come that they may have life, and that they may have it more abundantly." John 10:10 (NKJV)

THE TRADITION OF HANGING STOCKINGS was not a part of my childhood. But I made Christmas stockings for my three children after they were born, using a different form of needlework for each one. How I loved watching them on Christmas morning as they pulled out and examined the small gifts and treats one by one—or excitedly dumped the contents out all at once on the carpet. For my part, I always thought it was fun seeing the empty, flat, and somewhat shapeless stocking transformed into a bulging bag of treats waiting to be discovered.

I was delighted one year when my daughter gave beautiful velvet stockings to my husband and me embroidered with *Nana* and *PawPaw*. Now I view an empty stocking hanging on a fireplace (or wherever) as a beautiful picture of trusting Jesus. Sometimes I resemble that pre-Christmas-morning stocking. A feeling of emptiness tries to invade my mind; my emotions feel flat rather than balanced. I might even question the shape my life is taking. Then I remember that Jesus delights not only in providing for my needs but in showering me with blessings that bring a full life of joy and meaning.

I want to keep my heart and mind open to Jesus's Word and His guidance. Like a child who has hung up her stocking, I'm looking forward to how Jesus will fill my life with gifts and surprises all through the year. —DIANNE NEAL MATTHEWS

FAITH STEP: *Place a Christmas stocking or a sock somewhere you'll see it each day. Arrange a candy cane to stick out of the top as a reminder of the sweetness of Jesus's gifts in your life.*

ADVENT DAY 20 EVENING

Friday, December 19

You crown the year with Your goodness, and Your paths drip with abundance. Psalm 65:11 (NKJV)

"Who made the corn dip?" I asked, scooping a generous portion onto my plate. "It's my favorite appetizer."

"Me," my daughter said. "Did you make your fluffy orange stuff this year?"

"I sure did. The Creamsicle Salad is on the dessert table."

Casserole dishes and Crock-Pots covered the countertops in the kitchen and flowed onto folding tables in the living room. My family always fixed more food than we could possibly eat at our Christmas gathering. But we liked it that way, because we relished leftovers. The delicious abundance would feed us several extra times.

I notice abundance all around me in the holiday season. Part of it feels a bit negative—too much spending, too many gifts, too many activities, and yes, even too much eating. I watch those things in my life and try to maintain a healthy balance.

But the true abundance I sense at Christmas comes from Jesus. He gives me abundant hope that carries the promise of heaven (1 Peter 1:3-4). He provides abundant peace that goes beyond my understanding (Philippians 4:7). He fills me with abundant joy that can only be described as inexpressible (1 Peter 1:8). And He extends abundant love to me that never fails (1 Corinthians 13:8).

I'm whipping up another batch of fluffy orange stuff this morning, preparing for the next holiday celebration. Orange Jello, vanilla pudding mix, mandarin oranges, whipped cream—and a super-large helping of mini marshmallows, just for the sake of abundance.
—Becky Alexander

Faith Step: *As you make (or buy) your specialty dish this season, double the amount, and thank Jesus for His abundance.*

Saturday, December 20

Rejoice in the Lord always. I will say it again: Rejoice!
Philippians 4:4 (NIV)

SO MANY GOOD THINGS HAVE been discovered by mistake: Post-it notes, chocolate chip cookies, super glue, Velcro, penicillin, even pacemakers. All of these items have had a significant impact on the world in positive ways. Although my mistake a few years ago doesn't hold a candle to any of those discoveries, it still has had an impact on me in a deep and meaningful way.

After we had packed up the Christmas bins and stored them away in the attic, I found an overlooked Nativity snow globe on a side table. The hinges on the pull-down ladder we use to access our attic were broken, making it an ordeal to get up there. The effort didn't seem worth it for just one item. It was easier to just leave that snow globe out. I decided to put it in my office.

Every day, as I glanced at the Nativity inside that snow globe, it reminded me of the true meaning of Christmas—be it March or October. That constant reminder had me expressing gratitude for Jesus's birth each and every day. It helped me realize that I'd been compartmentalizing the joy and the gift of Christmas into the season of Advent.

In all the years since, I've made the conscious decision to leave that snow globe out and visible. When I gaze at the Nativity within it, Advent joy, love, and gratitude are reborn in my heart all year through. —CLAIRE MCGARRY

FAITH STEP: *Consider choosing one Christmas decoration that reminds you of Jesus's birth and leave it out year-round.*

SATURDAY, DECEMBER 20

And he said: "Truly I tell you, unless you change and become like little children, you will never enter the kingdom of heaven." Matthew 18:3 (NIV)

MY FAMILY HAS A LONG-STANDING tradition of driving around to see the spectacular Florida light displays for my son's birthdays, but last Christmas, it was different. A high school junior with a December birthday, my son Pierce plays varsity baseball, and his practice, workout, school, and social schedule is packed. Plus, he's a young man, and a characteristic teen, who mildly scoffs at our tradition. We had a party with his friends, but there was no outing to view holiday lights since they're much too big and too many to pile in the van.

On the other hand, my middle schooler, Isaac, and I are still enthusiastic and often drive around to see the lights during Advent. One night, Pierce happened to be available and somewhat grudgingly agreed to join us. We visited a nearby mansion whose owners spare no expense and allow people to walk around their grounds.

At first, Pierce was grumbling and the mood in the car was sour. Even cheerful Isaac was quiet! But I persevered, frankly childlike in my delight. No sooner had we started strolling the spectacular display than the atmosphere shifted, maybe because the very first vignette was a life-size Nativity. Who can stay grumpy before 140-watt baby Jesus? We had a great time!

Jesus invites all of us to be childlike to enter heaven, and I've come to believe it's true this side of paradise too. Life is simpler and more joyful as children. —ISABELLA CAMPOLATTARO

FAITH STEP: *Anytime you feel grumpy this season, consider a childlike activity: string popcorn, make paper chains, look at Christmas lights around town or online.*

Saturday, December 20

Suddenly a great company of the heavenly host appeared with the angel, praising God and saying, "Glory to God in the highest heaven, and on earth peace to those on whom his favor rests." Luke 2:13–14 (NIV)

I'M PART OF A CHRISTMAS carol loving family. Some of my best childhood memories consist of clambering out of Grandpa Blakeley's church bus to serenade his unsuspecting church members. All thirty-plus of us—aunts, uncles, grandparents, and cousins—would break into "Joy to the World," unleashing our voices toward the cold December sky. Front porch lights would flip on, and folks would spill out to listen. The glorious goodness was all around.

Now my caroling is more of a singular practice. The other morning, I cranked up my Christmas playlist in the living room, unleashing my voice toward the ceiling. My husband, Scott, who does not hail from a caroling family, was gracious. The first time he visited my family at Christmas and we broke into four-part harmony, he was stunned into silence. Now he joins in.

The birth of Jesus inspired a holy caroling session. The shepherds rejoiced (Luke 2:20) as the angels sang out. They shared the unexplainable wonder of the moment when heaven came to earth. "Joy to the world. The Lord has come!" When I sing along, I echo the angel chorus announcing the birth of the One who loves me most of all. The One who left the glory of heaven to make me a part of His family forever (John 6:38). Now that is glorious goodness!
—SUSANNA FOTH AUGHTMON

FAITH STEP: *Remember the glorious goodness that surrounds you today. Take time to sing your favorite Christmas carols and praise Jesus.*

LOVE

Away in a manger, no crib for a bed,
the little Lord Jesus laid down His sweet head;
the stars in the heavens looked down where He lay,
the little Lord Jesus asleep on the hay.

The cattle are lowing, the Baby awakes,
but little Lord Jesus, no crying He makes.
I love Thee, Lord Jesus, look down from the
sky and stay by my side until morning is nigh.

Fourth Sunday of Advent, December 21

"Be sure of this—that I am with you always, even to the end of the world."
Matthew 28:20 (TLB)

When my kids were growing up, I gave them a special ornament each Christmas, carrying on a tradition my mother started with me. My son married this year, so I decided it was time to pass his ornaments to him so he could put them on the Christmas tree in the home he and his wife were creating together. When it came time to decorate my tree, I separated his from the rest.

It was bittersweet to pick up each one and remember why I chose it. There was a Baby's First Christmas with his newborn photo. A tiny violin and miniature guitar for the years he started playing those instruments. Several sports ornaments, hunting and fishing ornaments, an ornament for chess. There was even an Anakin Skywalker with a lightsaber from his Star Wars days, and several we bought on family vacations. A few were broken beyond repair so I had to throw them away.

As a mother, it is hard to let go of my children's time "in the nest" even as I am excited and proud to watch them fly away to new adventures. It is a comfort to remember that one thing—the love of Jesus—never changes. His love goes with them and also stays with me. It doesn't break, wear out, or get lost. Jesus is with me, even after my kids move on. —Gwen Ford Faulkenberry

Faith Step: *Buy or make an ornament that reminds you of Jesus's love for you. Every year as you place it on your tree, thank Him that He never leaves, and never will.*

Fourth Sunday of Advent, December 21

And when they had come into the house, they saw the young Child with Mary His mother, and fell down and worshiped Him. And when they had opened their treasures, they presented gifts to Him: gold, frankincense, and myrrh. Matthew 2:11 (NKJV)

When I made the decision to give my life to Jesus after college graduation, I didn't feel like I had much to offer Him. I walked forward to the altar because I needed something *from* Him: forgiveness. My college days had been an emotional roller coaster. On one hand, there were wonderful moments of growth educationally, socially, and spiritually. On the other there were the temptations of campus life, and numerous opportunities to "show out" with seemingly few consequences. Deep in my heart, I knew I needed to get serious about Jesus, but I felt so hopeless sometimes that I didn't want to face Him. Out of shame, I wouldn't allow myself to just fall down and worship Jesus as these wise men did. They traveled hundreds of miles, scholars say, hoping to find Him, and they brought along very precious and costly gifts too. They weren't there to *get* anything but a glimpse of their Savior. On the contrary, I felt I had so much I needed to get from Jesus, and very little to give. As I've grown in my faith over the decades, I realize the one thing I have to offer Jesus, He already has: my heart. —Pamela Toussaint Howard

Faith Step: *Close your eyes and kneel, or imagine yourself kneeling, beside the Magi. As they present their precious gifts, open your empty hands and offer Jesus your hopeful, unfettered heart.*

Fourth Sunday of Advent, December 21

We love because he first loved us. 1 John 4:19 (NIV)

My sweet friend handed me the box. I felt my face flush. Jai was giving me a Christmas gift and I had nothing to give her in return. It was a moment where Jai genuinely wanted to bless me, but the embarrassment of being caught empty-handed was sucking the joy right out of it for me. All the while, the Holy Spirit was reminding me that Christmas is not about "giving to get" as my parents used to say. So, I graciously thanked my friend and walked away thinking about Jesus. How many times have I done this to Him? How many times has He intentionally just wanted to bless me, and I felt that I owed Him something in return, or that I didn't deserve it?

Jesus is God's perfect gift to me. Jesus freely loves me and allows me to choose whether or not I want to love Him back. There's never any guilt or coercion. His decision to be born as a baby, walk as a human, and die as a man paved the way for me to truly see what love really looks like. Jesus never loved me because He felt like He had to. He loved me because He chose to. His life modeled how mine can look now if I follow in the footsteps of His perfect love.
—Kristen West

Faith Step: *Plan to give a Christmas gift to someone you know cannot give you one in return. Pray for that person to feel Jesus's love with your simple gift.*

Monday, December 22

I thought about the former days, the years of long ago; I remembered my songs in the night. Psalm 77:5–6 (NIV)

I'M A PASTOR, AND ONCE a month my church leads worship at the Alzheimer's care facility in our small town. Our Christmas service is everyone's favorite. We sing songs and we read the Christmas story from Luke's Gospel. Because of their limited cognitive abilities, many of the residents at the facility don't really know where they are or what is happening. But much to my amazement, they all still know the Christmas story.

As I read from the Bible, I ask the residents to share their reactions. We laugh about Joseph forgetting to make reservations in Bethlehem. We wonder about what that night sky must have looked like as the angels visited the shepherds. Then together we share memories of Christmases past. I discover their childhood memories are some of the last to fade.

It also became apparent that music lingers a long time in the declining brain. As we sing the Christmas hymns, even those residents who can no longer talk join in and sing the songs: "Joy to the World," "Silent Night." The melodies usually bring tears to my eyes. There is so much love and faith in the room, I can feel Jesus in our midst. And even though many there are no longer familiar with the stories of their own life, they still remember His story. —HEATHER JEPSEN

FAITH STEP: *Spend a moment reminiscing with a friend or a family member about Christmases in your past. Tell them how Jesus was and is a part of your story.*

Monday, December 22

> *See what great love the Father has lavished on us, that we should be called children of God! And that is what we are!* 1 John 3:1 (NIV)

This past summer my oldest son, Jack, married his college sweetheart, Emmalyn. It was a day of joy and excitement. We carried that excitement with us into the holiday season. Our whole family met in Colorado the week between Christmas and New Year's. We were on our way to my folks' house.

The newlyweds flew in from Oregon. My husband, Scott, our sons Will and Addison, and I flew in from Idaho. Will's girlfriend, Heather, flew in from California. Then we all squished into a rental SUV that turned out to be far too small. We had so much luggage my dad had to meet us and help transport the bags.

The anticipation was high as we made the hour-long drive. Grandma and Grandpa's house was full of aunts, uncles, cousins, and good snacks. There were hugs all around when we arrived. The sounds of laughter wafted upstairs from the basement. Games were played. Ping-pong matches were won. We soaked up the joy of being together as a family.

Jesus has invited me to be a part of His family too. By His grace and mercy, He made a way for me to know His Father in heaven. He has lavished His love on me. He calls me His child. And one day, I am going to soak up the joy of being with Jesus for eternity. I wonder if there will be hugs all around when I arrive.

—Susanna Foth Aughtmon

Faith Step: *Thank Jesus for making a way for you to be a part of His family. Close your eyes and imagine His arms hugging you tightly.*

Monday, December 22

For the poor will never cease from the land; therefore I command you, saying, "You shall open your hand wide to your brother, to your poor and your needy, in your land." Deuteronomy 15:11 (NKJV)

I TOPPED MY HOT COCOA with a handful of marshmallows and sat down to scroll through social media for a few minutes. I paused on a post by my friend George.

"Christmas 1972, my family lived in the old farmhouse on Michael Road. No plumbing, no gas furnace, only wood heaters.... Dad was out of work that year, so even as kids, we suspected Christmas could be a tough time."

I took a sip of my cocoa and continued reading.

"On Christmas Eve, we heard squealing sirens and saw flashing lights. From a window, we saw a fire truck—with Santa's sleigh hitched behind—turn in our driveway. Santa climbed down and waddled to the front door. He pulled gifts for each kid out of his bulging red bag."

I'd known George since elementary school. I had no idea that his family struggled back then. But somebody realized it, and jumped into action. Someone noticed a need, bought presents, and asked Santa to deliver them—all while remaining anonymous to the recipients.

Maybe Jesus will choose me to be that person this December, the one who discovers a difficult situation and takes steps to help. I don't have a red suit with a furry white collar, but I'm always in for a heavenly assignment. —BECKY ALEXANDER

FAITH STEP: *Ask Jesus to show you who needs a little help and make it happen.*

Tuesday, December 23

This is real love—not that we loved God, but that he loved us and sent his Son as a sacrifice to take away our sins. 1 John 4:10 (NLT)

IT WAS A DIFFICULT DAY. I had to meet with a divorce mediator and see my ex-husband for the first time in weeks. I wanted to do right by him, our kids, and myself, and that seemed impossible. It felt like I might fall into a million pieces.

As I drove my youngest daughter to school, I saw several roadside signs. "Pray for Israel" prompted a discussion of why only Israel should have prayer, and another, "Worthy is the Lamb," we believed to be true based on the book of Revelation, but we thought it a little odd to proclaim to passersby who may have never read or even heard of the book of Revelation. Still another declared, "Jesus is the answer." None of these really resonated.

Then we came upon a church sign with the simple words "God loves you. So do we. Welcome all!" That little three-part sermon reminded me that I am loved and anchored me with its truth.

I dropped my daughter at school, then drove toward the mediation office, confident that I wouldn't fall into a million pieces. The Great Mediator loved me and my ex-husband. Nothing was impossible with Him. —GWEN FORD FAULKENBERRY

FAITH STEP: *What difficult person is Jesus asking you to love today? Make a sign to reflect your godly resolve.*

Tuesday, December 23

Do not conform to the pattern of this world, but be transformed by the renewing of your mind. Then you will be able to test and approve what God's will is—his good, pleasing and perfect will. Romans 12:2 (NIV)

WHILE DECORATING THE CHRISTMAS TREE with my children, I had a long-ago memory enter my mind. Mom was not happy with the Christmas tree. After my dad placed the tree in the corner of our living room, Mom complained it wasn't straight. When the tree was finally standing to her satisfaction, she whined that it had too many bare spots.

I remembered that I longed to remind Mom that a perfect tree was not what Christmas was all about. Now that I was a mom, decorating our Christmas tree was the highlight of the season for me. I directed the kids on the placement of our ornaments. They were too small to reach the top half of the tree, and I found myself taking the decorations from their hands to replace them where they looked best.

Had I become my mother? Not with words, but my actions showed that I was unsatisfied about not having a perfect Christmas tree. I was teaching my children the wrong lesson about Christmas, just as my mom had taught me. I took a step back and suggested I hand them the decorations while they put them on the tree.

When we had finished, our tree was only decorated halfway up. But it was perfect. Small hands had placed each ornament with love. —JEANNIE HUGHES

FAITH STEP: *Abandon your desire to have the perfect Christmas tree. This year, focus on Jesus and the love represented in your decorations.*

Tuesday, December 23

"See, I am sending an angel ahead of you to guard you along the way and to bring you to the place I have prepared." Exodus 23:20 (NIV)

Walking into our dance hall for their annual Christmas party, I looked forward to spreading some cheer. I planned on giving hand-painted angels to each of the staff members who served us, but I wondered if I should include Shannon, the bartender. Our group rarely visited the bar and when I interacted with her, she didn't seem friendly. However, it seemed wrong to leave her out.

Gathering up my nerve, I approached her and offered my gift. Tears welled up in her eyes. "I could use an angel right now. Thank you." Not wanting to pry, I offered to pray for her. She came from behind the bar to give me a hug. I was stunned by her reaction.

Later that evening while praying for Shannon, I wondered how many times I had missed seeing someone's struggle because I was blinded by a harsh attitude. I decided to add a prayer for myself: *Jesus, open my eyes, my hands and my heart to those who need You. Help me see them as You do so they can see You in me.*

At our next monthly gathering, I stopped by the bar to see how Shannon was doing. "I looked at your angel every day. Everything eventually worked out." I still wasn't privy to whatever she was dealing with, but I was happy to have helped. Well—me, an angel, and Jesus. —Gloria Joyce

Faith Step: *Give a smile, a compliment, or a token gift to someone who regularly serves you.*

ADVENT DAY 25 MORNING

WEDNESDAY, DECEMBER 24

I wait for the Lord, my whole being waits, and in his word I put my hope. I wait for the Lord more than watchmen wait for the morning, more than watchmen wait for the morning. Psalm 130:5–6 (NIV)

My family's younger dog, Boone, was the last of his litter to get picked. His picture on the breeder's website was uber cute in an elf hat and collar, and his eyes held sweetness. So, right before Christmas, we decided to add him to our family.

I wanted to pick up Boone on Christmas Eve and bring him home for the holiday. But because of the six-hour distance by car, we—and he—had to wait two more days.

He had experienced his littermates leave one by one, until little Boone sat alone in the kennel through Christmas Eve and the holiday.

We had chosen him but, I imagine, his hope was deferred.

At times I've felt as if a dream passed its expiration or that Jesus didn't come through on time. But the truth remains that Jesus is always working behind the scenes on my behalf, even when the provision tarries (Philippians 4:19).

The memory of Boone's excitement when we finally picked him up tugs at my heart each Advent season.

If Christmas Eve ushers in the holidays then passes without fulfilling a longing, I know Jesus is at work and is never late with His gifts. —Erin Keeley Marshall

Faith Step: *Write today's verse on a notecard and wrap it in a box. Open it the day after Christmas as a reminder that Jesus is always working and will provide.*

WEDNESDAY, DECEMBER 24

All right then, the Lord himself will choose the sign—a child shall be born to a virgin! And she shall call him Immanuel (meaning, "God is with us"). Isaiah 7:14 (TLB)

I'VE CELEBRATED CHRISTMAS EVE IN a variety of ways. I remember opening gifts with extended family all crowded in together at my grandparents' tiny house. We'd sing "Happy Birthday" to Jesus and eat cake Gramma had ordered from the bakery with "Happy Birthday, Jesus" written in frosting. We attended Midnight Mass. Then, when I was raising my own family, we had fun reading aloud a Cajun version of "The Night Before Christmas." After the kids went to bed, I'd stay up all night wrapping presents and filling Christmas stockings.

Sadly, Gramma's long gone, and now our kids are all grown and living on their own, far away. So my husband, John, and I have since adopted new Christmas Eve traditions in the little town where we moved to be near my parents. Inspired by the movie *A Christmas Story*, we started going out for Christmas Eve dinner with my parents to a Chinese restaurant (the only place open on Christmas Eve).

Now Dad's gone, and the old Chinese restaurant is no more. But that doesn't stop us from celebrating Christmas Eve with Mom. We still love attending Christmas Eve candlelight service together at our little neighborhood church. Though loved ones may be absent, Jesus is still with us. Immanuel! Now that's reason to celebrate! And, who knows, maybe next year I'll order a "Happy Birthday, Jesus" cake from the bakery. —CASSANDRA TIERSMA

FAITH STEP: *Take a moment to remember past Christmas Eve celebrations, then thank Jesus for being present for all of them.*

WEDNESDAY, DECEMBER 24

The light shines in the darkness, and the darkness has not overcome it. John 1:5 (NIV)

I LIVE IN ARKANSAS, AND one of the reasons I love it here is that we experience all four seasons. That is, I always think I love it until midwinter. That's when it gets darkest the earliest, everything is gray, and I want to escape to somewhere that is warm and green.

Victorian poet Christina Rossetti wrote "In the Bleak Midwinter" that characterized the world into which Jesus came:

In the bleak midwinter
Frosty wind made moan
Earth stood hard as iron
Water like a stone.

Whether it has ever been so cold in Bethlehem is questionable, but I think Rossetti, a devout Christian, meant something deeper than the literal darkness of midwinter. I think she looked out at the world and saw what we all see if we are honest. The beauty, which she puts in other poems, but also the darkness. The bleakness of irreconcilable differences, incurable diseases. The coldness of death and loss. The meanness of greed. The hardness of poverty and injustice. Rossetti saw and felt the weight of the world.

She also saw the overcoming of it, as she shows a few lines later:

In the bleak midwinter
A stable-place sufficed
Lord God Almighty, Jesus Christ.

The infinite love that birthed Jesus in that bleak stable-place is the same love that comes to be with us, even in our darkest places. Jesus is not overcome by darkness. Nor am I. —GWEN FORD FAULKENBERRY

FAITH STEP: *Light a candle and watch how its flame illuminates the darkness. Whisper, "Happy birthday, Jesus!"*

Thursday, December 25

When Jesus spoke again to the people, he said, "I am the light of the world. Whoever follows me will never walk in darkness, but will have the light of life." John 8:12 (NIV)

I COULDN'T WAIT TO DECORATE our new home for Christmas last year. I felt like a kid as I pawed through boxes of holiday décor that had been in storage for three years. I spent hours switching items from room to room, but problems with the lights frustrated me. Only half the lights worked on my small pre-lit tree. None of the lights for the front door garland and small front porch tree worked.

A few shopping trips later, I had replacements. For the final touch, I bought the perfect stars for our living room windows. I inserted batteries, hung them from suction cups, and pushed the "on" button. Only one of the two stars lit up with tiny fairy lights. And the store had none left in stock.

No wonder lights are such a vital part of the season that celebrates the birth of a baby born to redeem a darkened world from sin and death. As the Light of the World, Jesus sees all the dark shadows in my life that threaten me: fear, loneliness, past hurts. As sure as the bright star guided the wise men to Jesus, He invites me to follow His light. Christmas lights from a store will eventually quit working, but Jesus's light will never falter. —DIANNE NEAL MATTHEWS

FAITH STEP: *Step outside or stand near a window to bask in the light of this Christmas Day. Thank Jesus for shining His hope, peace, joy, and love into the dark areas of your life.*

CHRISTMAS MIDDAY

Thursday, December 25

"For there is born to you this day in the city of David a Savior, who is Christ the Lord." Luke 2:11 (NKJV)

EVERY YEAR AS I UNWRAP the Nativity, I play "what if I were this character" and wonder: How did Mary feel, gazing upon the face of Jesus, being the first to worship Him with a kiss? Did Joseph's emotions include not only the thrill of fatherhood but the overwhelming sense of responsibility he faced as provider for the Son of God? The shepherds circling the manger must have been filled with wonder and anxiousness. Could they also have comprehended the honor they'd been bestowed? Did the livestock sense the importance of the holy birth? The innkeeper, the angels—how did they experience the miracle of Jesus's sacred arrival from their perspectives? Every year, I consider where I stand in this cast. Sometimes I'm the lowly sheep, offering my trough for His bed, and other years I relate more closely with the innkeeper, a shepherd, or Mary herself.

As I gently set the porcelain figures in place, I'm reminded that instead of playing another character in this story, I've been invited to attend this blessed event as myself. I fall to my knees humbly, reverently, and gratefully as the words to "O Holy Night" come to mind, when "He appeared and my soul felt its worth." I'm graced with the "thrill of hope" and take part as the "weary world rejoices." For today, here in my quiet home and everywhere throughout the earth, "a new and glorious morn" is breaking. Christ is born!
—HEIDI GAUL

FAITH STEP: *Gaze at your Nativity and consider the varied characters God invited to Jesus's birth. With whom do you most identify?*

CHRISTMAS EVENING

Thursday, December 25

And the angel said to her, "Do not be afraid, Mary, for you have found favor with God." Luke 1:30 (ESV)

THE YEAR 2020 WAS A time of global and personal change for me. I'd just gotten divorced and was recovering from what seemed like the unjust bankruptcy of my business. I was ardently seeking God for answers and for whatever was next, so I started working with a spiritual director. Spiritual direction is a practice that originated with fifteenth-century theologian Saint Ignatius of Loyola as a means of discerning God's movement in our lives through prayer, scripture contemplation, and silent listening. One of the first exercises my spiritual director, Nancy, assigned me was meditating on Henry Ossawa Tanner's 1898 painting, *The Annunciation*, a beautiful, unexpectedly modern representation of Mary's encounter with the angel Gabriel, who tells the young maiden she'll give birth to Jesus, the King of an "everlasting kingdom."

Nancy invited me to imagine myself in the painting. To ask Mary what it was like for her. What she felt. What I felt. At first, my pragmatic, critical mind resisted this unfamiliar, mystical task, but I lingered on the eloquent rendering of Mary's life-changing moment. Suspending skepticism, I was deeply moved by what God revealed intimately to me. Like Mary, was I willing to serve Him however He asked?

Mary's humble willingness, embracing the countless uncertainties that awaited her, remains an inspiration to me. Today I'm mentally revisiting the exercise, a precious reminder both of Christ-mass, a celebration of holy communion with Jesus, and God's transformative invitation to follow the King into His everlasting kingdom.
—ISABELLA CAMPOLATTARO

FAITH STEP: *Find Tanner's* The Annunciation *online and put yourself in the painting. Savor the spiritual direction exercise by answering the questions for yourself.*

The Birth of Jesus

In those days Caesar Augustus issued a decree that a census should be taken of the entire Roman world. (This was the first census that took place while Quirinius was governor of Syria.) And everyone went to their own town to register.

So Joseph also went up from the town of Nazareth in Galilee to Judea, to Bethlehem the town of David, because he belonged to the house and line of David. He went there to register with Mary, who was pledged to be married to him and was expecting a child. While they were there, the time came for the baby to be born, and she gave birth to her firstborn, a son. She wrapped him in cloths and placed him in a manger, because there was no guest room available for them.

And there were shepherds living out in the fields nearby, keeping watch over their flocks at night. An angel of the Lord appeared to them, and the glory of the Lord shone around them, and they were terrified. But the angel said to them, "Do not be afraid. I bring you good news that will cause great joy for all the people. Today in the town of David a Savior has been born to you; he is the Messiah, the Lord. This will be a sign to you: You will find a baby wrapped in cloths and lying in a manger."

Suddenly a great company of the heavenly host appeared with the angel, praising God and saying,

> "Glory to God in the highest heaven,
> and on earth peace to those on whom his favor rests."

When the angels had left them and gone into heaven, the shepherds said to one another, "Let's go to Bethlehem and see this thing that has happened, which the Lord has told us about."

So they hurried off and found Mary and Joseph, and the baby, who was lying in the manger. When they had seen him, they spread the word concerning what had been told them about this child, and all who heard it were amazed at what the shepherds said to them. But Mary treasured up all these things and pondered them in her heart. The shepherds returned, glorifying and praising God for all the things they had heard and seen, which were just as they had been told. —Luke 2:1–20 (NIV)

Contributors

Becky Alexander 6, 52, 58, 66, 76
Susanna Foth Aughtmon 21, 29, 36, 69, 75
Laura Bailey 11, 37
Isabella Campolattaro 35, 53, 62, 68, 85
Pat Butler Dyson 12, 33, 41, 50, 59
Gwen Ford Faulkenberry 24, 57, 71, 77, 82
Heidi Gaul 20, 25, 47, 54, 64, 84
Pamela Toussaint Howard 31, 39, 72
Jeannie Hughes 17, 28, 43, 78
Heather Jepsen 46, 74

Gloria Joyce 19, 23, 44, 49, 79
Jeanette Levellie 15, 32, 38, 51
Ericka Loynes 56, 63
Erin Keeley Marshall 7, 14, 60, 80
Dianne Neal Matthews 10, 16, 65, 83
Claire McGarry 5, 30, 40, 67
Emily E. Ryan 9, 22, 27, 55, 61
Cassandra Tiersma 13, 34, 42, 81
Kristen West 8, 18, 45, 73

Acknowledgments

Scripture quotations marked (CEV) are taken from *Holy Bible: Contemporary English Version*. Copyright © 1995 American Bible Society.

Scripture quotations marked (ESV) are taken from *The Holy Bible, English Standard Version*. Copyright © 2001 by Crossway Bibles, a division of Good News Publishers. Used by permission. All rights reserved.

Scripture quotations marked (GNT) are taken from the *Good News Translation*® (Today's English Version, Second Edition) © 1992 American Bible Society.

Scripture quotations marked (HCSB) are taken from the *Holman Christian Standard Bible*. Copyright © 1999, 2000, 2002, 2003, 2009 by Holman Bible Publishers, Nashville, Tennessee. All rights reserved.

Scripture quotations marked (KJV) are taken from the *King James Version of the Bible*.

Scripture quotations marked (NASB) are taken from the *New American Standard Bible*®, Copyright © 1960, 1971, 1977, 1995, 2020 by The Lockman Foundation. All rights reserved.

Scripture quotations marked (NCV) are taken from *The Holy Bible, New Century Version*. Copyright © 2005 by Thomas Nelson. Used by permission. All rights reserved.

Scripture quotations marked (NIV) are taken from *The Holy Bible, New International Version*®, *NIV*®. Copyright © 1973, 1978, 1984, 2011 by Biblica, Inc. Used by permission. All rights reserved worldwide.

Scripture quotations marked (NKJV) are taken from the *New King James Version*®. Copyright © 1982 by Thomas Nelson. Used by permission. All rights reserved.

Scripture quotations marked (NLT) are taken from the *Holy Bible, New Living Translation*. Copyright © 1996, 2004, 2007, 2015 by Tyndale House Foundation. Used by permission of Tyndale House Publishers Inc., Carol Stream, Illinois. All rights reserved.

Scripture quotations marked (NLV) are from the *New Life Version of the Bible*, copyright © 1969, 2003 by Barbour Publishing Inc.

Scripture quotations marked (TLB) are taken from *The Living Bible*. Copyright © 1971 by Tyndale House Publishers, Inc., Carol Stream, Illinois. All rights reserved.

A Note from the Editors

We hope you enjoyed *Walking with Jesus: Devotions for Advent & Christmas 2025,* published by Guideposts. For over 75 years, Guideposts, a nonprofit organization, has been driven by a vision of a world filled with hope. We aspire to be the voice of a trusted friend, a friend who makes you feel more hopeful and connected.

By making a purchase from Guideposts, you join our community in touching millions of lives, inspiring them to believe that all things are possible through faith, hope, and prayer. Your continued support allows us to provide uplifting resources to those in need. Whether through our communities, websites, apps, or publications, we inspire our audiences, bring them together, and comfort, uplift, entertain, and guide them. Visit us at guideposts.org to learn more.

We would love to hear from you. Write us at Guideposts, P.O. Box 5815, Harlan, Iowa 51593 or call us at (800) 932-2145. Did you love *Walking with Jesus: Devotions for Advent & Christmas 2025*? Leave a review for this product on guideposts.org/shop. Your feedback helps others in our community find relevant products.

Find inspiration, find faith, find Guideposts.

Shop our best sellers and favorites at
guideposts.org/shop
Or scan the QR code to go directly to our Shop